Happy holidays,

Martin

W9-BYN-425

PRAISE FOR

BUBBLES

AND HOW TO SURVIVE THEM

"Financial bubbles have always exercised a fascination over academics and financial journalists. Business economists can make their reputation by spotting them in time. But in truth relatively little is known about what generates bubbles, what causes the eventual bust, what damage bubbles can do, and how they can be prevented. Most importantly, are we in one now?

In this book, John Calverley explores this subject in considerable depth, using an analytic approach but writing in a style accessible to the interested layman. Calverley is the Chief Economist of American Express bank, so he knows what he is talking about. He belongs to the school that believes bubbles are recognisable, dangerous and preventable. Moreover, he thinks the housing market in Britain and some other countries now displays the characteristics of a bubble. He has a number of policy recommendations, many of which will prove controversial.

Not everyone will agree with all aspects of his diagnosis or prescription. But it is hard to dispute that this book addresses an important and so far poorly understood topic."

Sir Andrew Crockett, President, J. P. Morgan Chase International and former General Manager, Bank of International Settlements, 1999–2003

"This is a must read for anyone considering investing in housing or stocks as well as market practitioners wishing to glean insights into how the herd can behave."

Gerry Celaya, Chief Strategist, Redtower Research

"This is an indispensable book for everyone, investors and students alike, who wants to understand how bubbles arise—and to avoid being caught out by the next one."

Roger Bootle, Capital Economics

"This book offers a timely warning. Around the world real estate prices have been rising strongly as home-buyers take advantage of low mortgage rates. But if home price increases turn out to be a bubble, the consequences for many recent buyers as well as for the economy as a whole could be severe."
Ranga Chand, economist and expert on mutual funds, Toronto

"There is no more controversial question that what to do about the housing bubble, whether you are a buyer, a seller, a renter or a central bank governor. John Calverley has compiled a primer for all, tackling the many difficult questions logically and informatively. He is to be commended for making some very constructive proposals for what looks like a problematic future."
Alex Erskine, Managing Director of Erskinomics Consulting, Visiting Fellow with Macquarie Applied Finance Centre, Sydney and former head of Asian research for a leading global bank

"A clearly written analysis that deftly uses statistical data to reveal the nature of bubble/bust cycles and offers insights on how to deal with them."
Tadashi Nakamae, Nakamae International Economic Research

"Calverley has written a book for our times: when growth is fuelled by asset bubbles and central bankers held hostage by the fear of their collapse. He brings a global view and the lessons of economic history to diagnose the problem, to develop new ideas for policy makers and to provide sound advice for investors."
Dr. DeAnne Julius CBE

"If you are worried about your future, read this book with care. If you're not, read and take heed. This is high quality, X rated stuff, not for the faint-hearted, written with great clarity and balance. Essential reading on any public financial education course."
Richard O'Brien, Partner, Outsights

BUBBLES

AND HOW TO
SURVIVE THEM

The data, facts and examples used in this text are believed to be correct at the time of publication but their accuracy and reliability cannot be guaranteed. Although the author expresses a view on the likely future investment performance of certain investment instruments, this should not be taken as an incitement or a recommendation to deal in any of them, nor is it to be regarded as investment advice or as a financial promotion or advertisement. Individuals should consider their investment position in relation to their own circumstances with the benefit of professional advice. No responsibility is assumed by the author or the publisher or American Express Bank Ltd. for investment or any other decisions taken on the basis of views expressed in this book.

American Express Bank Ltd., 60 Buckingham Palace Road, London, SW1W 0RR (No. FC 1863, BR301). Incorporated with limited liability in the State of Connecticut, USA and registered with the Secretary of State, Hartford, Connecticut, USA with its head office in New York, USA.

BUBBLES
AND HOW TO
SURVIVE THEM

John Calverley

NICHOLAS BREALEY
PUBLISHING

LONDON   BOSTON

First published by
Nicholas Brealey Publishing in 2004

3–5 Spafield Street
Clerkenwell, London
EC1R 4QB, UK
Tel: +44 (0)20 7239 0360
Fax: +44 (0)20 7239 0370

100 City Hall Plaza, Suite 501
Boston
MA 02108, USA
Tel: (888) BREALEY
Fax: (617) 523 3708

http://www.nbrealey-books.com

© American Express Bank 2004
The right of John Calverley to be identified as the author of this work
has been asserted in accordance with the Copyright, Designs and
Patents Act 1988.

ISBN 1-85788-348-9

British Library Cataloguing in Publication Data
A catalogue record for this book is available from the
British Library.

All rights reserved. No part of this publication may be reproduced,
stored in a retrieval system, or transmitted, in any form or by any
means, electronic, mechanical, photocopying, recording and/or
otherwise without the prior written permission of the publishers.
This book may not be lent, resold, hired out or otherwise disposed of
by way of trade in any form, binding or cover other than that in
which it is published, without the prior consent of the publishers.

Printed in Finland by WS Bookwell.

CONTENTS

Foreword   ix
Preface   xi
Introduction: Why Bubbles Matter   1

PART I BUBBLE AND BUST   9

1   An Anatomy of Bubbles   11
2   The Great Depression   26
3   Japan and the Specter of Deflation   42
4   The Greenspan Bubble and Reflation   57

PART II HOUSING: THE NEXT CRASH?   71

5   The Worldwide Boom   73
6   Britain Nears the Top   84
7   A US Bubble?   97
8   Household Debt and Monetary Policy   107

PART III ORIGINS AND SOLUTIONS   121

9   The Pathology of Bubbles   123
10   Valuing Markets Sensibly   137
11   New Policy Approaches   159
12   Strategies for Investors   181

Final Thoughts: Living with Bubbles   195
Notes   203
Index   215

FOREWORD

There can hardly ever have been a more timely book than this. Asset price volatility, and especially the movement of house prices, has moved center stage in the economy. A central theme of the book is that asset bubbles make the economy, and possibly the financial system, potentially unstable. In this regard, John Calverley has addressed one of the key issues and risks of the day and argues persuasively of the danger of a period of debt deflation and a serious risk that house prices could fall sharply as a bubble in the market is burst. The combination of record high levels of debt and a housing bubble also increases the risk of monetary policy mistakes.

In a carefully chronicled *tour de force*, which is written in a wonderfully clear and engaging style, John Calverley has produced a powerful insight into some of the many myths that surround this subject, and most especially the housing market. The author gives us some fascinating insights from behavioral finance and in particular into how markets can lose touch with reality.

Everyone has an interest in this subject and Calverley has produced a book that can be easily read by both technicians in the subject and the layperson. It deserves to be very widely read.

David T. Llewellyn
Professor of Money and Banking, Loughborough University

PREFACE

In recent years a series of bubbles and busts in the world's stock and property markets have become the main focus for both investors and policy makers, overshadowing the much milder fluctuations in ordinary consumer price inflation. Many investors lost heavily in the collapse of the 1990s stock bubble, but now many people are betting on continually rising house prices. Meanwhile, policy makers seem to have no way to restrain bubbles; indeed, their adherence to orthodox policies may be making the problems worse.

This book looks at bubbles from two points of view: those of the interested observer of the economy and the investor. In truth, most of us are both. The performance of the economy matters to everyone, through its impact on jobs and incomes. But the performance of asset prices from an investment point of view is more important than ever, for the value of our homes and for our security in retirement.

The US is the most critical arena, by virtue of its own importance and because America's economic health remains vital for the whole world. Moreover, US monetary policy has played a central role in bubbles everywhere in the last two decades. However, Britain and Australia are currently leading the way in the housing bubbles and I also draw heavily on experiences in Japan and Hong Kong.

The Introduction sets out the key problem we face today. Federal Reserve Chairman Alan Greenspan led the way in cutting interest rates to contain the fallout from the 1990s stock market bubble, but at the cost of inflating huge, and potentially even more dangerous, housing bubbles. Policy makers now have to find a way to normalize interest rates and maintain economic growth, without triggering either a collapse in house prices and a new recession, or alternatively a return to high inflation.

The first part of the book looks at how bubbles emerge and the effects they have on the economy, both as they inflate and when they collapse. The 1920s stock market bubble, very similar in many ways to the 1990s experience, is analyzed to see how and why we avoided disaster this time, though the full consequences of the 1990s bubble are still working through, with pensions in crisis and many investors retaining unrealistic expectations for returns. Japan's 1980s bubble and bust are examined, with particular emphasis on the interaction with deflation, a consequence of the bust but also a major impediment to recovery.

Part II looks at the emerging housing bubbles around the world. While the UK and Australia are extreme cases, US home prices are already bubbling in some regions and, unless price increases slow, most of the country will soon be affected. Household debt has risen rapidly alongside housing bubbles and the implications for stability and for monetary policy are explored.

Part III looks at the underlying origins of bubbles and offers some solutions. Studies in the field of behavioral finance show how investors sometimes lose touch with reality. If this is allied with policy mistakes the combination can be lethal. The key issue of valuations is addressed: Can we identify "reasonable" levels for markets, so that investors have better warning of when bubbles are developing and policy makers can consider countermeasures? And what countermeasures are available, for example through monetary policy, public warnings, or "speed limits" on bank lending? The last chapter looks at strategies for investors, who must try to avoid bubbles or, more dangerously, seek to ride them.

Finally, I offer some thoughts on how the twin problems of housing bubbles and rising debt will evolve. Much will depend on monetary policy and whether central bankers can be astute enough, and perhaps lucky enough, to find their way through. Major adjustments will be necessary in the US economy and others. If the adjustments can be made gradually and smoothly, the outcome will be fine. If they occur abruptly, it could be a rough ride.

My interest in bubbles goes back to university days and I owe a great debt to four teachers in particular: Michael Kuczynski, Hyman Minsky, and David Felix, who always emphasized the role of financial market instability, and Larry Meyer, who placed the emphasis on intelligent policy making to deal with crises. As a practicing economist and strategist in the 1980s, my interest was kindled with the 1987 stock market crash, the subsequent bubbles in housing, and, most of all, the bubble and bust in Japan. When the US stock market took off again in the second half of the 1990s and the Asian bubble collapsed, I resolved to write this book. It has taken a long time and the stock bubble has been replaced by housing bubbles—but the issue is more relevant than ever.

ACKNOWLEDGMENTS

I am enormously grateful for comments and suggestions from Kate Barker, Roger Bootle, Claudio Borio, Gerry Celaya, Alex Erskine, Jan Hatzius, DeAnne Julius, Richard O'Brien, Mark Tapley, David Walton, and Sushil Wadwani. Also to many colleagues at American Express, including Bob Friedman, Kevin Grice, Sarah Hewin, Dan Laufenburg, Gordon Townsend, Chris Wang, and Meiping Yang. Sharon Thornton and Maria Whittaker have helped with tables and charts.

I also want to thank Nicholas Brealey. Never before have I experienced such an active publisher. His suggestions, while often challenging, have always been stimulating and have made the book much more readable than if I had been left to my own devices!

Finally, I would like to thank American Express Bank for encouraging me to write this book. However, the views expressed herein are entirely those of the author and are not necessarily those of American Express Bank Ltd. or its affiliates.

INTRODUCTION:
WHY BUBBLES MATTER

Most people have heard of the Tulip Mania (Holland, 1630s), the South Sea Bubble (London, 1720), and the Wall Street Crash (the US, 1929). Less well known are the emerging market mining mania (London and South America, 1820s) and the railway mania (UK 1840s), and there were many more in the eighteenth and nineteenth centuries.[1] These were all bubbles: a huge rise in prices followed by a crash.

In the middle decades of the twentieth century there was a lull, when bubbles were few and far between. But in the last 20–30 years bubbles have returned in a big way. In the last quarter of a century we have had the Japanese bubble (1980s), the UK and Scandinavian housing bubbles (late 1980s), the Asian Tigers bubble (mid-1990s), and the technology mania (late 1990s). Not only are they giving investors a roller-coaster ride, they are also having a major impact on the economy.

In each case the story begins with a rise in prices in the market in question, often for a good reason, which then continues on upward to an extraordinary level of valuation, before crashing back. On the way up the rise in price encourages a high level of business investment, boosting economic growth and prosperity and often creating a sense of euphoria. Following the crash the economy is hit by a combination of reduced wealth, financial caution, and uncertainty. At best this brings only an economic slowdown or a mild recession. At worst it can create a major depression, as in the US in the 1930s or Japan in the 1990s.

That such patterns repeat is a source of wonder to many. Does this mean people have short memories? Does it mean they are irrational? Is there a flaw in the financial system that encourages speculation? Kindleberger, in his classic 1978 book on the subject, was forced to argue at some length why contemporary commentators, who argued that the world had changed and bubbles had become less likely, would be proved wrong.[2] He was writing in a period when the world had been relatively free of major manias and crashes for a while. Now, with the collapse of the 1990s stock market bubble still reverberating and amid signs that housing bubbles are emerging, the old patterns have returned with a vengeance.

Earlier systems of economic organization, such as feudalism, nineteenth-century capitalism, or socialism, involved a sharp concentration of economic wealth and power in the hands of a few landowners, a small group of capitalists, or an elite group of bureaucrats. Today, ownership of assets is much more widespread. Even 50 years ago only a very small proportion of the population held any assets other than small-scale deposits. Now more than 75 percent of the population in developed countries own stocks, mutual funds, houses, or pensions.

It is also much easier to trade assets than before. The immediate transparency of prices on electronic quotation systems is now accessible to all through the internet, whereas just a few years ago it was available only to the big financial institutions. Even the purchase of property, still a relatively illiquid asset, has become easier, with the internet reducing search costs and mortgages more readily available.

The new asset-backed economy creates a far wider dispersion of wealth and represents a genuine democratization. But it also brings volatility, which can be very damaging to the economy as well as creating crippling losses for investors.

TWENTIETH-CENTURY BUBBLES

The most disastrous bubble ever seen was the 1920s US stock bubble. After it burst in the Wall Street Crash of 1929, the effects of the asset price collapse, combined with central bank and government policy mistakes in 1931–2, plunged the world into a severe depression. The resulting political turmoil, particularly in Germany and Japan, combined with trade protectionism to lead ultimately to the Second World War.

The worst episode in recent times has been in Japan following the collapse of its stock and property bubbles. From the peak in 1991, land

2

prices fell more than 90 percent while stock prices slumped 80 percent. The 1990s was a "lost decade" for Japan, with economic growth averaging less than 1 percent a year and unemployment rising sharply. Interest rates were cut too slowly to kick-start the economy and attempts to use active fiscal policy led to an explosion of government debt. And, though the government has avoided a banking crisis, it has yet to deal fully with the overhang of bad debt left from the bubble years. Hopes are high that the economy is at last making a genuine recovery, although it has been a very long time coming.

In 1997–8 the Asian Tigers suffered a similar crisis, after asset price bubbles collapsed. While the trigger was a currency collapse, it was the massive rise and subsequent fall of property and stock prices that made the aftermath so painful. Only a few years earlier, as the bubbles inflated, these countries had been enjoying what was widely regarded as the "Asian miracle."

Today we are living with the aftermath of the 1990s stock bubble, fostered by technology and growth stocks. In the late 1990s US policy makers, led by Federal Reserve Chairman Alan Greenspan, sat back and watched as the US stock market went into a bubble strikingly similar to the 1920s experience. They argued that it was not necessarily a bubble and that, even if it were, it would be dangerous to deflate and much better to wait and be ready to deal with any bust after the event.

Whether allowing a bubble to inflate unchecked is really the best approach remains a controversial question, examined carefully in the pages that follow. What is clear, though, is that having learned the lessons from the 1930s and also the 1990s Japan experience, the US authorities have been determined to prevent the asset price bust leading to a major economic slump and deflation. So far at least they have succeeded, with the help of rapid and deep cuts in interest rates and a huge fiscal stimulus. The US did suffer a recession in 2001 but it was only comparatively mild. And the economic recovery picked up steam in 2003–4, so that fears of deflation have receded. Nevertheless, reactive policy is creating new difficulties for the future.

BUDGET DEFICITS

The budget stimulus instigated by President Bush, including major tax cuts and increased military spending, was the largest fiscal stimulus in American history. But the legacy is a budget deficit of more than 5 percent of GDP, a level that creates problems of its own for the long term. European countries have also used active fiscal policy in recent years, particularly the UK but to a lesser extent Germany and France as well, and deficits are now running in the 3–4 percent of GDP range, again too high.

High deficits drag on economic growth, by reducing the resources available to the private sector and raising real interest rates. They also threaten rising government debt ratios, which can eventually make debt unsustainable. Japan already faces this problem with its debt ratio at over 160 percent of GDP. The US and Europe still have ratios closer to 60 percent (the UK at only 40 percent), so their problem is less urgent. However, this is not the whole story because governments have additional liabilities that are not included in official debt data, the most important being pensions and health care.

So far the US has avoided the drag from its budget deficit with the help of a matching current account deficit. In effect, foreigners are financing the budget deficit by sending the money gained from their trade surpluses with the US straight back into the US economy. During 2003–4 Asian central banks were the main sources of finance, buying US dollars to prevent their currencies appreciating too much so that they could maintain their own economic expansion.

Nevertheless, this large current account deficit also has long-term consequences for the US, in the build-up of foreign liabilities. At some point the current account deficit will need to be corrected and this will imply a prolonged period of dollar weakness. A weak dollar will help the US economy if the problem then is maintaining growth, but is a threat if inflation should start to pick up again. This will depend on whether or not the US has spare resources in the economy at the time.

High budget deficits have another important consequence. If we face a new economic slump, governments will have used up their fiscal ammunition. Japan reached this point in the mid-1990s, five years after the bust began, but the US and Europe got there in just two years. In the US the authorities used up virtually all their monetary policy ammunition too, taking interest rates down to 1 percent. Provided that the current economic recovery continues, rates will rise in the next few years but, in a world of low inflation, will remain relatively low. There are other monetary measures that can be taken if rates hit the zero limit, but these are untried and untested.

The US stimulus succeeded in averting an economic disaster in 2002–3 partly because of its sheer size and speed of implementation, but also because of a crucial difference between the 1990s bubble and Japan's experience. Japan's bubble was not only in stocks but in property too. When property prices fell in the 1990s the effect was to undermine Japanese companies' balance sheets and leave banks with huge losses.

In contrast, property prices in the US and Europe held up fairly well after the stock market bust. Commercial property prices were relatively restrained in the 1990s and when economic growth slowed in 2001 there was only a limited overhang of supply, so rents and prices were only moderately affected. But—and this is critical—residential house prices not only have not fallen but, most unusually during an economic downturn, have risen sharply.

By cutting interest rates so dramatically, there is a danger that central banks have shifted the bubble from stocks to residential property. I shall argue that, with valuations at historically high levels, we face housing bubbles now in the UK, Australia, Spain, and the Netherlands. Worryingly for everyone, a bubble may be emerging in the US as well. If these bubbles give way to busts there is a risk that the next recession will be severe, especially since the evidence suggests that property price declines have more impact on the economy than stock price falls. Moreover, with inflation so low, there is a danger that a new recession in the next few years could see more countries following Japan into a deflationary scenario. While deflation is not always bad news, it is something to fear if asset prices are falling too and debt is high. With household debt at record levels in all these countries, the potential for serious problems is considerable.

WHY BUBBLES MATTER

When any bubble goes bust, some people lose. Experienced speculators can be caught out, though they sometimes recognize the end of a bubble and cut their positions in time. Most importantly, they usually know how to limit their risk to a bearable level. The investors who really suffer are those who are drawn in, often at the late stages of a bubble, with very little experience of how to manage risks.

For a bubble to continue to inflate it needs more and more people to invest, risking more and more money. The end of the bubble occurs either because there is nobody left to be drawn in, or because some event makes people start to sell.

If bubbles affected only a few investors, with little impact on the overall economy, they would be of limited importance. Some bubbles are indeed like that. The bubble in classic car prices in the late 1980s, for example, had only minor repercussions. A few people made a lot of money on the way up and some lost when prices crashed at the end of the decade, but the numbers involved were small. Obviously classic cars cannot be newly manufactured so, although there were some new dealers who set up during the bubble and then closed after the bust, the wasted resources involved were small. The bubble in impressionist paintings at the same time had a similarly limited effect, as did bubbles in silver and gold prices in the 1970s.

However, bubbles can cause major problems when they occur in an asset that is widely held. Then, not only do a large number of people suffer directly when the bubble bursts, as the bubble inflates it also interacts with the economy, creating a self-reinforcing boom and bust. The dangerous bubbles, therefore, are usually the ones in stocks and property.

POLICY DILEMMAS

So what can be done? Can we find ways to prevent bubbles inflating? Are there clear warning signs, from valuations or other factors? Should we look for ways to restrain bank lending when prices become too much out of line? And how can investors protect themselves?

These are the issues that will be discussed in Part III of this book. First, we need to take a look at the origins and effects of previous bubbles in Part I, and particularly at the problem of housing bubbles in Part II.

PART I

BUBBLE AND BUST

1 AN ANATOMY OF BUBBLES

T he valuation of assets plays a crucial role in the market economy. A rise in the price of one asset relative to another encourages resources to flow in that direction, whether we are talking about technology shares, houses, or tulip bulbs. But private markets also seem periodically to lose themselves in wild speculation and then equally wild pessimism: bubbles followed by busts.

The classic profile of a bubble involves several stages.[1] In the beginning there is a so-called displacement, some outside event that changes the investment landscape and seems to open up a new opportunity. The displacement can be the end of a war, a new technology (canals, railways, the internet), or perhaps a large fall in interest rates. The nature of the displacement is the biggest source of variation between bubbles, and perhaps this is one of the causes of the problem. We are unlikely to see a second internet bubble, but who knows what new technology in the future could generate similar excitement?

If this displacement effect is strong enough, it generates an economic boom as investment goes into the new area. Often banks play a major role in fueling the bubble by accommodating a rapid expansion in credit. But history suggests that even if existing banks are not major participants, other sources of credit and finance come to the fore, including new banks, other types of finance companies, foreign banks, personal credit, and so on. New investment floods into the booming sector, pushing up prices and opening up still more profit opportunities.

At some stage the bubble reaches a phase variously called euphoria or mania, where speculation mounts on top of genuine investment and expectations for potential returns reach wild heights. Strong market performance is extrapolated endlessly forward and any consideration of fundamental valuation criteria is swept aside. More and more people are drawn into speculation, in the hope of making quick money. It is at this point that taxi drivers talk about the market; near the final peak everybody's mother wants to buy too! Generally you find numerous people warning of a bubble, sometimes politicians and bankers, at other times newspaper writers. Nevertheless, their first warnings are usually too early and they often become discredited.

Eventually the market rise slows as some people take profits and fewer people are willing to come in. Sometimes there is a period of eerie calm, before a new event precipitates a decline in prices. This event can be a new external shock such as a war, or it may be a rise in interest rates or a slowdown in the economy as new investments have come on stream and it has become evident that there is overcapacity. The trigger does not necessarily have to be a large event; sometimes it is simply "the straw that breaks the camel's back."

The next stage is called "revulsion": prices fall, financial distress rises, bankruptcies mount, and banks pull back on lending. The economy is affected by the fall in new investment and the rise in uncertainty so that perfectly good projects now fail, adding to the distress. General business confidence evaporates and everybody wants to "wait and see" before committing to new hiring or fresh investments. Consumers may also hold back on large purchases such as cars or houses, concerned that their jobs are at risk as well as their investments.

There may also be a "panic" phase, when prices fall extremely rapidly as people try to sell before everyone else and there are hardly any buyers. Liquidity may dry up. Prices fall precipitately, in a kind of reverse speculation. Eventually, either they fall so far that people decide they are now cheap, or the authorities close the market for a while hoping for the panic to subside, or use some kind of "lender of last resort" activity to restore confidence. However, it is rare to escape this phase without at least a serious economic slowdown and usually a recession.

IDENTIFYING BUBBLES

The description above is the typical pattern of a bubble in outline. In my view, it is comparatively easy to recognize a bubble when it is fully or nearly fully inflated, though some people dispute even this and argue that a bubble is only definitely confirmed afterwards, when it has burst. For an investor, recognizing a bubble is crucial if potentially large losses are to be avoided. From a public policy perspective, in terms of managing the economy it would be useful to identify a bubble or potential bubble early, before it reaches extreme valuations.

Table 1.1 presents a checklist of typical elements that have been observed in bubbles from the South Sea to the internet. Most of these are very obvious at the height of a bubble, though in the earlier stages it is more a matter of judgment.

Table 1.1
Checklist: Typical characteristics of a bubble

○ Rapidly rising prices
○ High expectations for continuing rapid rises
○ Overvaluation compared to historical averages
○ Overvaluation compared to reasonable levels (see Chapter 10)
○ Several years into an economic upswing
○ Some underlying reason or reasons for higher prices
○ A new element, e.g., technology for stocks or immigration for housing
○ Subjective "paradigm shift"
○ New investors drawn in
○ New entrepreneurs in the area
○ Considerable popular and media interest
○ Major rise in lending
○ Increase in indebtedness
○ New lenders or lending policies
○ Consumer price inflation often subdued (so central banks relaxed)
○ Relaxed monetary policy
○ Falling household savings rate
○ A strong exchange rate

Source: Author, partly based on "Bubble trouble," *HSBC Economics and Investment Strategy*, July 1999.

RAPIDLY RISING PRICES

First of all, a bubble obviously involves a period of rapidly rising prices. However, a strong rise in prices in itself does not necessarily imply a bubble, because prices may start from undervalued levels. So we should only start to suspect a bubble if valuations have moved well above historical averages, on indicators such as the price–earnings ratio for stocks or the house price–salaries ratio for housing. The extent of this overvaluation probably gives us the best clue as to the exact probability of a bubble. For example, the US stock bubble in the 1990s took the price–earnings ratio on operating earnings (which excludes one-off factors) to over 30 times, well above the long-term average of about 14–16 times (see Chart 1.1).[2]

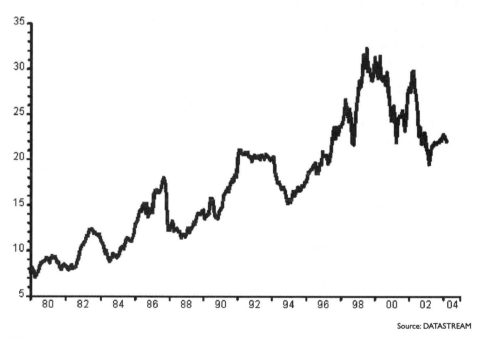

Source: DATASTREAM

Chart 1.1
US S&P 500 price–earnings ratio

OVERVALUATION

The issue of valuation is contentious, with many people arguing that we can never be sure that a market is really overvalued. I disagree and believe that we can identify ranges for valuations that are more or less reasonable, such that if a market goes above them, we can say that there is at least a high probability that it is a bubble. Further evidence can then be sought in other characteristics.

ECONOMIC UPSWING

Typically bubbles develop after several years of solid, encouraging economic growth and rising confidence. The traumas of past recessions and bubble crises (at least in the same market) have faded away. For example, the US 1990s stock market bubble came in the last three years of a nine-year economic expansion and following fifteen years of a relatively strong stock market. And the Asian property and stock market bubbles that burst in 1997–8 came after over a decade of breakneck expansion, which had become known as the Asian Miracle.

The current housing bubbles are a little different in that they have inflated at the same time as the collapse of the stock bubble. However, they come 10 years or more after the last housing bubble burst in the early 1990s and they are partly the result of the low interest rates put in place to fight the effects of the bursting of the stock bubble. Moreover, the most intense housing bubbles currently are in Australia, the UK, and Spain, three of only a handful of major countries that avoided a recession during 2000–3.

NEW ELEMENT

As noted earlier, another typical characteristic of a bubble is a new development or change in the economy that can reasonably justify higher prices. In the 1990s it was computers and networking technology and, more broadly, the apparent sharp acceleration in US productivity growth that led to much talk of a "new economy." In the 1980s in Japan it was the perception that the Japanese economic model, with all its panoply of "just-in-time" inventory management, worker involvement, and "total quality control," was going to dominate the world. Current housing bubbles in the UK and Australia are often linked to increased immigration.

PARADIGM SHIFT

There is often the perception of a "paradigm shift" and this is usually argued energetically by some leading opinion formers. We shall see later that people seem to have an innate tendency to believe (or want to believe) that current events are entirely different from any episodes in the past. This is a natural characteristic of younger people especially and certainly the 1990s internet boom was very much led by young people. But of course, some people have a vested interest in arguing that "it is different this time"—especially brokers, fund managers, and real estate agents.

I do not for one moment want to sound like someone who has seen it all before and believes that nothing is new under the sun. Economic performance and market behavior do change over time and periods of strong performance and weak performance can persist for a long time, often decades or more. Nevertheless, it is dangerous to extrapolate this into justifying very high valuations, at least without serious caveats.

Even if higher valuations in a market can be justified by fundamental changes in performance, we should expect this to be a one-off move, not a shift to permanently faster price increases. For example, faster growth of profits would justify higher valuations, but once valuations have moved a step higher, stock price gains should then slow down to the rate of growth of profits. It is unrealistic to expect valuation multiples to expand further. The same goes for house prices. If a higher house price–earnings ratio really is justified now, as many people argue, once the step higher has been made house price growth should return to the growth rate of earnings.

The US 1990s experience is interesting in this regard. The acceleration in productivity growth in the 1990s, part of the paradigm shift that accompanied the bubble, continues to be reaffirmed. US productivity growth since 2000—that is, after the bubble—has averaged 4 percent a year, a very high rate. Similarly, the new technologies continue to permeate the economy in ways that many of the new economy enthusiasts correctly predicted. But during the bubble a crucial point was forgotten: Faster productivity growth does not mean higher profitability in the long run. At first it brings higher profits, but this then brings more investment, more competition, and, eventually, lower

16

prices so that the gains flow through to increased real incomes. Profits fall back to normal levels because in a market economy companies cannot hold onto them in the long run.

NEW INVESTORS AND ENTREPRENEURS

Returning to the checklist, a regular feature of bubbles is that new investors are typically drawn in, people who had not invested at all before or had been only very passive players. They are persuaded by the bulls' arguments and also by the continuing rise in the market. Often they are assisted by the emergence of new entrepreneurs, for example those offering new investment vehicles, like the internet offerings in the late 1990s or the buy-to-let funds in Britain and Australia in recent years.[3]

POPULAR AND MEDIA INTEREST

Popular interest in the market becomes intense and this is reflected in greatly increased media coverage. Some stories emphasize the "wow" factor, as big rises in markets make people rich overnight. During stock bubbles, media stories may be tinged with envy for the lucky few, or even hostility toward "speculators." In the case of housing markets, where often a majority of readers will be gainers, the emotional hook may be glee at the good news. A subtext may be that the reader too can get rich and some coverage will put the emphasis on how to join the party, for example providing information on stock funds or on mortgages and property investment.

Another type of media story will focus on the risk that the market is in a bubble, warning of trouble and usually critical of speculators and, sometimes, of the authorities for allowing it. There are nearly always some commentators who forecast the demise of the bubble. For example, in the late 1990s *The Economist* and the *Financial Times* regularly returned to the bubble theme in US stocks. In recent years they have been justifiably pleased with themselves, although too polite to gloat. And they have turned their attention to warning about housing bubbles.

MAJOR RISE IN LENDING

Typically bubbles also involve a significant rise in lending by banks or other lenders. Sometimes this reflects regulatory or structural changes in lending practices and often it involves new entrants to the market. The housing bubbles in the UK and Scandinavia in the 1980s followed the liberalization of banking systems, which allowed banks to lend far more freely than in the past. Debt tends to rise and the household savings rate tends to fall. Behind all this is often what I would characterize as a relaxed monetary policy. Sometimes this is evident from a rapid rise in money growth. Probably more important, though, is the rate of credit growth; that is, the increase in debt (related to but not identical to the rate of money growth). Sometimes too it can be seen in the level of real interest rates in the economy, which may look unusually low.

STRONG EXCHANGE RATE

A final characteristic of most bubbles is a strong exchange rate or, if the currency is fixed, an inflow of resources. During the bubble money flows into the country, either attracted by the booming asset or drawn in by the strength of the accompanying economic boom. The strong currency then leads to trade and current account deficits. Indeed, that is the "purpose" in a sense, so that there can be a net capital inflow, by definition equal to the current account deficit.

Not all of the items on the checklist are present in every bubble. Ultimately, deciding whether a particular market boom is really a bubble is a matter of judgment, based on the number of characteristics present and how extreme they have become. If we think back to the internet bubble of the late 1990s, it should have been clear to all at the end of 1999 and the beginning of 2000 that this was a bubble. But by then the bubble was nearing the peak, with the US NASDAQ index rising from about 2,800 at the beginning of October 1999 to its peak of just over 5,000 six months later. It dropped back through the 2,800 level in December 2000 and went to a low of about 1,200 in 2002, the same level as 1996; see Chart 1.2. Ideally we would have identified a high degree of bubble risk as early as the middle of 1998 and some degree of risk also in 1997.[4]

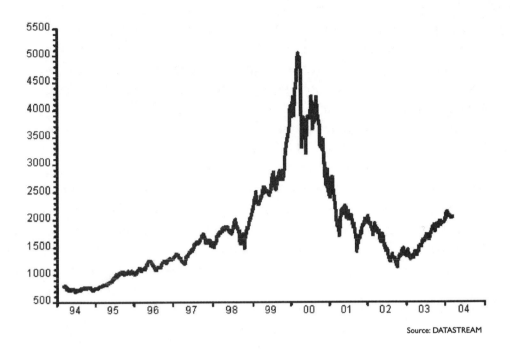

Source: DATASTREAM

Chart 1.2
The NASDAQ bubble

BUBBLES AND CONSUMER SPENDING

People respond to rising asset prices through so-called wealth effects. Small movements in asset prices may have little effect, but if the rise in wealth is large enough then, after a while, some people change their behavior. If the stock market has soared, perhaps they cancel their regular savings plan and use the money to go out to dinner more often, boring their friends with their skill in picking stocks. Others may take some profits and use the proceeds to buy a new car or a boat. If house prices rise fast they may increase their mortgage to spend money on a new kitchen or a home extension.

Some might say that people are foolish and shortsighted if they immediately spend gains. But many people have a target level of wealth and, if asset price inflation enables them to reach it earlier than they expected, why not spend more? After all, for most people the purpose of acquiring assets is for spending at some point. Of course, if the increase in prices is temporary and later reverses, they will be in for a rude awakening. There is also a danger that, after a period of price gains, they start to expect continuing gains at the same pace and adjust their spending further upward.

The evidence suggests that most people do not immediately spend gains but in fact respond only gradually. Possibly they are slow to realize that they are better off. Or perhaps they take a cautious approach to higher asset prices and only spend the gains when they believe that they are permanent. There is a potential trap there, though. The judgment as to whether or not higher asset prices are permanent tends to be based more on whether prices hold up for a while rather than whether valuations make sense. But as a bubble inflates, prices often exceed sensible valuations for an extended period and people start to see those high levels as normal.

Another common response to higher asset prices is to increase borrowing to finance higher spending. In the US it is relatively easy for people to borrow against stocks, even with only modest stock portfolios. In other countries often only those with a large portfolio can directly borrow against stocks, though there are other ways to take leveraged positions, including CFDs (contracts for differences), ETFs (exchange traded funds), and, in the UK, spread betting.

Still, for the average person, borrowing against assets is far more likely to be in the form of "mortgage equity withdrawal" (or MEW), as house price gains are released by remortgaging. Over the last 20 years it has become much easier to do this in many countries as rules have been relaxed, either through further advances or through switching mortgages and increasing the amount.

If the money raised from borrowing against assets is used to fund spending, then the effect is a fall in the household savings rate and it is this change in the savings rate that is the measure of the wealth effect. The savings rate is calculated as the difference between current income and current spending, and therefore ignores the fact that the increased spending may only be possible through new borrowing or sales of assets.

A crucial point to note here is that a fall in the savings rate only has a one-off effect on the *growth* of spending. Imagine a couple who respond to a rise in the value of their house by cutting their regular savings plan from 10 percent of their annual income to 5 percent. As a result there is a one-time 5 percent increase in their spending that year and a 5 percent drop in their savings rate. But the following year, if they stick to the 5 percent savings plan, their spending will only change in line with their income.

This creates a tricky problem for monetary policy, because central bankers are very much focused on the growth of the economy. If everybody in the economy cut their savings rate by 5 percent at the same time, there would be a sudden leap of 5 percent in consumer spending. This would immediately set alarm bells ringing and create fears that the economy was growing too fast and that higher inflation would follow. The response might well be to raise interest rates to try to calm things down. But the next year consumer spending growth would drop straight back to its old growth rate. If central bankers fail to realize what is happening, there is a real danger of a monetary policy mistake, with interest rates set too high.

The risk becomes even greater if people finance the extra spending from borrowing or from sales of assets, rather than from changing their regular savings, because in both these cases the extra spending will actually be reversed the following year. Suppose consumers raise enough cash through sales of assets to increase their spending one year by 5 percent. Next year, unless they repeat the exercise, they have only their income, so spending will register a *fall* of 5 percent. The central bankers are even more at risk of getting it wrong.

Sometimes people respond to rising wealth by taking on more debt to finance new asset purchases. One common reaction is to buy a second home, perhaps selling some stocks for a downpayment but also taking out a new mortgage. In this case there is no change to consumer spending or the savings rate or to consumers' overall wealth (after subtracting the new debt). But total assets are up, debt is higher, and the consumer has more risk. Meanwhile, home prices are likely to rise further, pushed up by the new demand.

Fortunately, some people are more cautious in response to higher asset prices. For example, a risk-averse response is to sell some stocks to pay off debts. Others may respond to rising house prices by remortgaging with a larger loan, using that debt to pay off other (higher-interest) loans, or by increasing deposits, against a rainy day. Again, risk is reduced. If debt is paid off, as in the first case, then risk is certainly reduced. In the second case though, the individual's overall wealth is still dependent on house prices holding up. And from the point of view of central bankers there is still the worry that, one day, those extra deposits will be spent.

All the effects described above go into reverse if asset prices fall enough to seriously reduce wealth, so that savings rise as a percentage of income. This last happened in the 1970s when the ravaging effects of inflation on real wealth encouraged a rise in the savings rate as people tried to restore their balance sheets. But also, when asset prices fall, people often get scared and want to reduce their risk, by paying off debt or switching out of riskier assets such as stocks. Of course, this is not the best moment to do so and indeed may be exacerbating the asset price cycle. Nevertheless, many people are impelled to reduce their risk.

CALCULATING WEALTH EFFECTS
Economists have tried to calculate the size of these wealth effects in practice. This is not easy, because rising asset prices usually coincide with rising incomes and falling unemployment, both of which also encourage spending. Moreover, to some extent rising asset prices and rising spending may both be the result of a monetary stimulus from the central bank, via a fall in interest rates. Nevertheless, despite all the caveats, most of the research finds that there is a measurable effect on consumer spending from higher asset prices, but that it varies from country to country.[5] A few studies failed to find any wealth effect from stock markets and a very few found that house prices were not very significant either. However, most find house prices more important than stock prices, with the effect up to twice as great.

Research in this area goes back to the 1970s and in the US a rule of thumb has emerged saying that for every one dollar increase in asset values, consumers will spend 5 cents more. Most subsequent studies for the US seem broadly to support this figure, though it is perhaps better to think of a range of from 3–7 cents.[6] The link between asset prices and consumer spending seems to be greater in the US than in continental Europe. Americans are generally more influenced by stock prices since more than half of the population own stocks, either directly or through mutual funds, while an increasing number of employees have 401K pension accounts.[7]

Sometimes it is argued that stock market wealth effects may not be very important in the economy because stockholdings are concentrated among the top 10 percent or so of earners. The trouble with this argument is that so is a large part of consumer spending. In Britain stocks probably have less direct impact, though there are substantial indirect holdings in pensions and insurance policies. But housing prices in Britain are very volatile during the economic cycle and this has historically been very important, as we shall see later.

In continental Europe, stock markets are generally much smaller in relation to GDP, with companies relying more on banks for finance. And in some countries, Germany and France for example, house prices have been rather less volatile than in the UK, often because the financial system or tax structure discourages easy buying of houses. In countries where the financial systems are liberalized, as in Scandinavia in the 1980s or the Netherlands and Spain in the 1990s, there have been substantial bubbles. Intriguingly, one study that found only very limited stock market wealth effects did find them for the US, Ireland, and Finland. These are the three countries with the most dramatic stock market booms in the second half of the 1990s.[8] This would appear to confirm the idea that wealth effects may not matter very much in normal times, but can become very important during extreme movements.

BUBBLES AND COMPANY BEHAVIOR

For companies it is stock bubbles that matter and it is the value of their own share price that is particularly important. When their own share price is high, the value of new investments to expand the company will appear to be high relative to the cost of making them. This approach has given rise to a measure of stock market valuation called Tobin's Q, after economist James Tobin. Tobin's Q is the ratio of the market value of a company to the replacement cost of the company if it had to be recreated by investing anew. It can also be used to value the whole stock market and Q for the US market reached around 2 times at the peak in early 2000, compared with a historical average of 0.7.

There is some doubt over how accurately Tobin's Q can really be measured because it depends on having good data on the current cost of past investments, something of a gray area in accounting. Moreover, defenders of high valuations argue that such calculations fail to properly account for the value of intangible assets such as brand names, or the "human capital" accumulated within a company, the practical experience of running the business. Nevertheless, if the ratio rises as much as it did in the 1990s, the chances are that the market is becoming overvalued.

To illustrate Q, imagine a company called WhizzPizza that owns a chain of 100 pizza restaurants and also has $2 million in cash reserves. WhizzPizza is quoted on the stock market and the market currently values the company at $102 million. So the market is valuing the average restaurant at $1 million. Now, if WhizzPizza calculates that the total cost of starting a new restaurant is only $500,000, it should spend the cash to start four new ones as soon as possible, because afterwards the company will be valued at $104 million. Tobin's Q is 2 in this example. If, however, it would cost $2 million to get one new restaurant started (Q of 0.5), it would be better to give the $2 million back to the shareholders, since a new pizza restaurant would lower the value of the company to $101 million by investing (101 outlets but the cash is spent).

It is easy to see how companies' responses to asset price signals can reinforce the economic cycle by exaggerating investment when the economy and stock market are booming and depressing investment during an economic downturn. Facing a Q of 2, WhizzPizza has an enormous incentive to borrow as much as it can and also to raise new equity in order to expand. But eventually, there will be so many new pizza restaurants (started both by WhizzPizza and its competitors) that the return from each one will start to fall. When the value of a new one falls into line with the cost of setting it up, Q has fallen to 1 and, at this point, investment slows because the pizza market is effectively saturated.

This pattern plays out regularly in individual markets as new products go through a life cycle that eventually reaches saturation. However, if Tobin's Q is high across the whole stock market, the effect is a widespread investment boom that also, eventually, produces a degree of saturation. Once investment slows across the whole economy, economic growth slows, contributing to the slowdown phase of the economic cycle.

The most damaging bubble of all time was the 1920s US stock bubble, which interacted with the economy in a disastrous way, leading to the Depression. Following the Wall Street Crash of 1929, US GDP fell by an incredible 30 percent and unemployment rose to 25 percent. The 1990s bubble was similar in many ways to that in the 1920s and stock ownership is more widely spread over the population now than then, through direct holdings and pension schemes. But, so far at least, the 1990s bubble has not brought disaster. In the next chapter we look closely at what went wrong in the 1930s as a prelude to analyzing what is happening now, after Greenspan's bubble.

2 THE GREAT DEPRESSION

M ajor bubbles are usually associated with a boom in the economy and busts are associated with a recession or even a depression. But what is the main direction of causation? Association does not prove causation and the linkages clearly go both ways. Economic booms drive stock and house prices up while economic slowdowns usually send them down again. But rising stock and house prices help to generate those economic booms while asset price busts hurt spending.

If stock or house prices move first, before the economy, we cannot simply assume that they must be the main causal factor. For one thing it is natural that markets, particularly stock markets, should move in anticipation of economic changes, as people buy stocks because they correctly see higher profits coming. But that puts the causation the other way around. There is also a possibility that asset price moves and economic fluctuations are both the result of a third causal factor, namely monetary policy. For example, a period of low interest rates will stimulate asset prices by encouraging people to move money out of low-yielding deposits into other investments and then, usually slightly later, stimulate the economy too. Conversely, a tight monetary policy hits asset prices first and the economy later.

In my view all these linkages play a role to some extent. Asset prices are both a cause and a consequence of economic developments, and they are also a consequence of monetary policy. The relative importance of the linkages and the most important directions of causation vary at different times and in different places. And economic policy, especially monetary policy, can have a major impact.

The 1920s bubble was followed by the most terrible depression in history, while the 1990s upswing has brought only the mildest of recessions. In the center of today's story is Alan Greenspan, Chairman of the

Federal Reserve Board. He took the conscious decision not to try to prick the bubble in the late 1990s (in contrast to his predecessor) and then to pull out all the stops to provide monetary stimulus once the bubble burst. His approach undoubtedly owed something to the lessons from Japan in the 1990s. But Greenspan is a keen student of history and, of course, is old enough to have experienced debates on these issues at least from the 1940s, when they were still very fresh in people's memories. So his decision not to follow up on his famous "irrational exuberance" speech of 1996, when he criticized investors, must at least partly have been conditioned by his reading of the 1920s and 1930s.

THE ROARING 20S

The story begins with the Roaring 20s, which in many ways uncannily resemble the 1990s.[1] The 1920s, like the 1990s, constituted a period of economic boom combined with a stock market bubble, but without any sign of general inflation. Also like the 1990s, there was much excitement about the new technologies of the time, as well as a growing sense of comfort as the decade progressed that the (then newly established) Federal Reserve Board could control the business cycle and avoid a major recession. One important difference, to which we will return, is that the 1920s saw a rapid growth in real estate prices, both residential and commercial, whereas real estate prices in the 1990s rose only moderately, with investors concentrating on stocks and perhaps still chastened by the falls in property prices in the early 1990s.

The sudden end of the First World War in 1918 had brought a sharp recession in 1919–21 as the economy adjusted. But 1922–9 saw a period of extremely rapid growth, with GNP up on average by 5.5 percent a year. Unemployment came down from 11 percent at the height of the postwar recession to 3.5 percent in the second half of the 1920s. Consumer prices were relatively stable, though GNP growth varied sharply from year to year with strong growth in 1922, 1923, 1926, and 1929 and relatively slower growth in the intervening years.

The economy was driven by new investment opportunities arising primarily from three new technologies: electric power, telephones, and automobiles. Although all three of these inventions date back to the end of the nineteenth century, it was in the 1920s that their use became sufficiently widespread to play a broad role in the economy. Investment was stimulated through increasing production but also because the greater use of these technologies required new spending. Increased car usage required investment in roads, services and supply centers, and oil refining. It also encouraged the growth of something relatively new at the time—suburbs—which drove a surge in house building. There is a parallel here with computers, which, although invented in the 1940s, only began to play a major role in the economy from the 1980s onwards.

There was also much excitement about another new technology at the time, radio, which was only just emerging and did not really play much of an economic role until the 1930s. It was, however, a strong sector in the stock market, with Radio Company of America (RCA) the dominant player, as both the leading manufacturer of radios and the leading broadcaster. Its stock price rose from $1½ in 1921 to a high of $114 in 1929, 73 times its earnings. Radio in the 1920s was the equivalent of the internet in the 1990s, a major stock market area with lots of capital flowing in, but little economic impact until a few years later. Two other technologies, aircraft and movies, also created great excitement. Charles Lindbergh's solo crossing of the Atlantic in 1927 stimulated interest in companies such as Wright Aeronautical, Curtiss, and Boeing Airplane. Meanwhile Hollywood was making the transition from silent movies to talkies and profits were rising rapidly while the large studios were consolidating.

With unemployment low, wages rising, new products available, and profits rising, a heady "feel-good" factor emerged. The stock market rose, modestly at first, but in 1926 it began to accelerate. Share prices rose 2.2 times between March 1926 and October 1929, driven by strong profits, the apparently increased stability of the economy, and confidence in the future. The same pattern occurred 70 years later with the US S&P 500 index rising moderately in the early 1990s, but then tripling between 1995 and 2000.

Taking 1921–9, the average annual rise in the market was 18 percent. This compares with an annual rise in the S&P 500 index of 15.5 percent per annum from 1990–2000. Investment trusts, long established in Britain, became very important in the US and, moreover, were allowed to use substantial leverage. In 1928 over 200 new investment trusts were launched with combined assets of over $1 billion. Three years earlier the combined capital of investment trusts had been less than $0.5 million. Land and property prices also rose strongly in the 1920s, with outstanding mortgages up from $11 billion in 1920 to $27 billion in 1929. Finally, consumer borrowing took off in the 1920s through "installment lending," enabling Americans to buy assets such as refrigerators and cars on credit.

As is typical of a bubble, there was much talk of a new era. This was partly a reflection of the eight years of expansion and general prosperity. But observers at the time also felt optimistic because of several novel factors. One was the creation of the Federal Reserve Board in 1913, which, it was believed, would be able to act as lender of last resort to banks, thereby avoiding the panics of the past that had often exacerbated economic slowdowns. Another was the extension of free trade following the First World War and with much of the world at peace. We can perhaps see a parallel here with the collapse of the Berlin Wall in 1989, which ended the Cold War.

Another positive factor cited at the time was the new "scientific" style of corporate management associated with the rise of large companies and particularly Henry Ford's production line. This was expected to even out inventory swings, which were recognized as one of the main causes of business cycle fluctuations. The claim that the inventory cycle had been tamed, this time by computer technology, reemerged in the 1990s; though, in the event, the 2001 recession saw one of the sharpest inventory corrections ever.

As is usual in a bubble, much of this optimism was reasonably based. For example, the 1920s did see a strong rise in productivity, up around 50 percent between 1919 and 1927. And the establishment of the Federal Reserve should have helped to reduce the impact of banking crises. The long-established Bank of England had learnt how to use its "lender of last resort" powers more than half a century earlier to avoid systemic banking crises, though it had certainly not been able to abolish the business cycle. However, as we shall see below, when the crisis came in the early 1930s, the Federal Reserve failed abysmally to prevent a banking crisis. Finally, the new products, including cars, the telephone, electricity, and radio, were indeed pivotal to life in the twentieth century. And they were also all "network technologies," like the internet.

During his successful election campaign in 1928 Herbert Hoover said: "We in America are nearer to the final triumph over poverty than ever before in the history of any land... We shall soon, with the help of God, be in sight of the day when poverty shall be banished from the nation." Most Americans agreed with him.[2]

MONETARY POLICY IN THE 1920S

Rapid economic growth, driven by strong investment, combined with declining unemployment and surging share prices, represented all the usual characteristics of a boom, with one exception. There was no general increase in consumer prices. The reason for this was partly the gold standard, which kept a brake on prices. But the strong investment itself, and the consequent increase in capacity combined with rapid productivity growth, also helped to hold inflation in check. In the 1990s a rapid growth of new investment had a similar effect. Inflation picked up only marginally near the end of the decade but still stayed at under 2.5 percent per annum, measured by the consumer expenditure deflator (Alan Greenspan's favorite inflation index).

The Federal Reserve was therefore not concerned about inflation in the 1920s and, until early 1928, monetary policy was highly accommodative. The Federal Reserve cut interest rates in 1925 to help the Bank of England return to the Gold Standard. In Britain this policy was instigated by Winston Churchill, then Chancellor of the Exchequer, in a bid to return to the stability of the pre-1914 world and avoid the risk of hyperinflation, which had ravaged Germany in 1923–4. However, the return to gold at the prewar rate, despite much higher wages and prices than in 1914, condemned Britain to deflation. The policy was initially resisted by Churchill himself and was vehemently criticized by John Maynard Keynes at the time, although it did reflect the prevailing orthodoxy.³ The immediate result was the General Strike of 1926 when workers unsuccessfully tried to resist cuts in wages, but the enduring result was that Britain enjoyed only lackluster economic growth during 1925–9 and largely missed out on the Roaring 20s.

Partly because of the overvalued pound, Britain was at risk of an outflow of gold and the cut in US interest rates in 1925 was designed to combat this. In the Summer of 1927 rates were cut again (partly also at French and German urging), taking the Fed's discount rate to a historic low of 3.5 percent. There is a parallel here with the US experience in the late 1990s when the Asian crisis in 1997, the Russian and Long Term Capital Management crises in 1998, and then worries over the Millennium Bug in 1999 kept interest rates low.

Returning to 1928, although the Fed was still not concerned about inflation it was becoming increasingly worried about the stock market gains. It started to raise interest rates in early 1928, believing that the stock market was too speculative and that the economy was in danger of overheating. However, rate increases were gradual rather than abrupt, because the Fed did not want to cut off the expansion. But higher US interest rates almost immediately began to reduce outflows from the US and, through the Gold Standard system, forced tighter monetary conditions elsewhere. The result was that the whole world started to see an economic slowdown in 1929.

There is little doubt that the buoyancy of asset prices in the 1920s reinforced the economic boom by encouraging business investment and consumer borrowing. Balance sheets expanded as risk seemed to recede and people set assets against new borrowings. Banks took on more risk and, especially in 1927–9, the stock market became a major focus for making money. Stock market trading houses proliferated, rather like the growth of on-line brokerages in the 1990s.

WHAT COULD HAVE BEEN DONE?

What should the authorities have done about the rise in share prices in the 1920s, if anything? Arguably the worst thing to do was to prick the bubble when it had already inflated—as seems to have happened on this occasion. By that time too many borrowing and spending decisions had been taken based on the high prices. It would have been much better to have deflated the bubble earlier. In their comprehensive study of US monetary policy, Milton Friedman and Anna Schwartz argue that "a vigorous restrictive policy in early 1928 might well have broken the stock market boom without its having to be kept in effect long enough to constitute a serious drag on business in general."[4]

Perhaps this is what happened when tighter monetary policy in early 1987 led to the stock market crash of October that year. Although the US did suffer a recession three years later in 1990, it is not likely that the stock market crash was the cause since the market by then had moved up to a new high. And there was only limited distress as a result of the crash because prices had shot up over a period of only about six to eight months. The market ended 1987 more or less where it began, but then proceeded on up gradually, with periodic modest interruptions, until 1995.

In the 1920s the Fed governors could not agree on whether or not there was a bubble and whether they should move against it. A major debate, on market valuations and on whether or not to act, raged within the Federal Reserve during 1927–8 and was not fully resolved until later in 1928, by which time the market had moved up substantially more. We cannot be sure that more aggressive rises in interest rates would not simply have brought forward the economic slowdown, but perhaps it would not have turned out to be so severe.

An alternative might have been to let the stock market rip in the 1920s. With no sign of consumer price inflation, why worry? Some commentators believe that the Federal Reserve made a mistake in trying to prick the bubble and should have merely left it.

However I, for one, believe that the bubble would still have burst, though perhaps a little later. It is impossible to know whether the result would have been better or worse than history records. But if the market had risen even higher it would then have had even further to fall, so it is certainly conceivable that the economic slowdown would have been even worse.

Another view is that the US market was not in a bubble at all in 1929 but fairly valued. This opinion was famously stated by Irving Fisher, a prominent economist at the time. A headline in the *New York*

Times on October 22nd, 1929, two days before the crash, claimed: "Fisher Says Prices of Stocks Are Low." Fisher continued to defend his view during the 1930s. Those who take this line imply that, without the Fed policy mistake of raising interest rates and slowing economic growth, there would have been neither a stock market crash nor a major economic slowdown.[5]

The assessment of whether or not stocks were fairly valued depends on a view of the prospects for the economy and profits, linked to a view of what is a satisfactory price–earnings ratio given that view. Taking the second point first, while there are differing estimates of the price–earnings ratio on the US market just before the crash, a reasonable estimate seems to be about 20–22 times earnings. One of the difficulties in making this assessment is that during a strong economic upswing profits may be inflated above their trend levels, both by the strength of economic activity and sometimes also by "optimistic" or even dubious accounting. Hence the estimate of 20–22 times may be a little on the low side.

In the late 1990s price–earnings ratios rose much higher than this, over 30 times earnings in 1999–2000. However, compared with the rest of the twentieth century, the 1929 level was already unusually high. The long-term average is around 14–15 times, with a range of about 8–20. The low ratios usually occur during major recessions and wars and the high ratios during strong economic upswings. The ratio in 1929 therefore reflected anticipations of continued good news on the economy and rapid profits growth. The ratio in 2000 at the peak of the 1990s bubble was even more bullish.

Was a buoyant view of the outlook realistic in 1929? As already stated, inflation was low so the economy was not yet under threat from an inflation problem (which at that time would have manifested itself in an outflow under the Gold Standard, automatically slowing the economy). However, economic upswings can come to an end due to "real" forces in the economy, not only financial factors (i.e., interest rates). The upswing would probably have run out of steam of its own accord sooner or later, most likely due to overinvestment. On this view, the Wall Street Crash did not cause the economic slowdown at all, but merely responded to it.

Given the frenzy in 1927–9, it is likely that some of the business investment of that period was a waste of resources (or at best premature), just as some of the investment in the 1990s proved to be. Hence I believe we can argue that, if the authorities had found a way to restrain the markets and avoid the excessive overvaluation of the 1920s, the outcome for the economy, and for most investors, would have been better.

What can we conclude, then, about the relationship between monetary policy, the Crash, and the economic slowdown? First, the rapid economic growth of the late 1920s as well as the stock market boom most likely had their roots in over-easy monetary policy from 1925 onward; that is, interest rates too low. Secondly, the policy of gradually raising interest rates from early 1928 onward led to a slowdown in the US economy that was clearly visible by the summer of 1929. Thirdly, while it does seem fair to blame the Fed for its excessively easy policy during 1925–7, we cannot be sure whether it had a better alternative in 1928–9. More rapid rises in interest rates might have curbed the market without upsetting the economy, but this is not certain. A slower path for interest rate hikes would have run the risk that stock prices rose even higher in 1929–30 or beyond. Finally, though this is anticipating the next section, we should not assume that the Fed's monetary policy in the 1920s created the Depression. Here researchers are generally agreed that it was monetary policy in 1931–2 where the big mistakes were made.

ALTERNATIVES TO MONETARY POLICY

What about alternatives to monetary policy to restrain the 1920s bubble? Governments and central banks can use other ways to restrain markets, including public warnings and limitations on lending. In fact the Fed did try hard to restrain margin lending, one of the drivers of the market. For example in February 1929, it warned its member banks that it did not consider brokers' loans a suitable use for funds. But, as Chancellor notes, "one reason margin loans proved intractable was that they were increasingly supplied by American corporations and foreign banks, neither of which were responsive to the Federal Reserve."[6]

In principle, margin lending can be better controlled now because in 1934, as a response to the 1929 Crash, the US government set up the Securities and Exchange Commission (SEC) to regulate brokerages, among other tasks. Similar organizations exist in other countries, for example the Financial Services Authority (FSA) in the UK, and margin lending is more strictly controlled than in 1929. However, in a strong bull market enthusiastic stock buyers can still borrow to buy stocks. Hedge funds can often leverage substantially too, though banks are somewhat more cautious since the collapse of LTCM in 1998. Investment trusts can use leverage, as with the UK Split Capital Trusts scandal in the late 1990s. But a modern phenomenon is the ease with which even ordinary people can borrow, particularly if they use housing as security. True, not many people deliberately increased their mortgage in the 1990s to buy a stock portfolio (though some probably did). But many did increase their mortgage, or other loans, ostensibly to buy consumer durables while simultaneously buying stocks or mutual funds. Though the two decisions may not have been directly linked, the purchase of stocks might not have taken place without the increased cash from borrowing.

THE 1930S DEPRESSION

At the end of 1929 the Fed was initially pleased with the breaking of the stock market bubble but, recognizing that the economy was weak, cut the discount rate sharply so that within a year it fell from 6 percent to 2.5 percent. At the same time fiscal policy was expansionary, as the government allowed the deficit to expand. Also, at the instigation of the government, wage maintenance agreements were put in place to try to prevent a downward spiral of wages and consumption.

This policy response was timely and wise and was generally thought to have been enough to contain the economic downturn to a moderate scale. Monetary and fiscal policy in 2001 proved remarkably similar, with a decline in the Federal funds rate from 6.5 percent to 1.75 percent and a major fiscal stimulus from the new Bush Administration. Wage maintenance agreements are no longer fashionable but, in any case, wages are not as flexible downward as they were in the 1930s.

A year or so after the Crash, in late 1930 and early 1931, some observers thought that the worst for the economy was over. December 1930 department store sales were almost back to their January level and they began to rise early in 1931. Unemployment had risen sharply, but the rate was only 1 percentage point higher than the peak seen in the previous downturn in 1922 (which was sharp but not a depression). The stock market at end 1930 stood at about half the peak October 1929 level, though only back to its end 1927 level.

However, a new economic decline developed in mid-1931 and took the economy down to the depths of 1932–3. During the same period the stock market more than halved again. This new downturn was precipitated by international events, beginning with the sterling crisis of April 1931. In September 1931, facing a weak economy and rising unemployment, Britain abandoned the Gold Standard and gold began to flow out of the US. The Federal Reserve responded in the classic way under the Gold Standard by reversing its easy money policy and tightening credit. This led to new stock market declines, a rush for liquidity, and a wave of bank failures. In 2002–3 by way of contrast, US interest rates were reduced a little more, to 1 percent.

The worst point of the Depression came in March 1933, when the wave of bank failures led to a general panic and the closure of all banks. The Dow Jones index actually bottomed before then with the close on July 8th, 1932 at 41.88, a drop of 90 percent from its peak. And RCA stock, the radio company trading at $114 in 1929, fell to just $3. The economy itself was in meltdown. GDP was down a massive 30 percent at its low in March 1933, with industrial production off by nearly 45 percent. Fixed investment fell to less than one fifth of the level of 1929 and comprised about half of the decline in total spending. Unemployment rose from 3.2 percent in 1929 to 25.2 percent in 1933. Consumer spending eased back in 1930 as the savings ratio rose, and then fell further in 1931–3 under the influence of weaker incomes.

Other countries around the world also suffered severe downturns, though generally less extreme than the US. Germany was one of the worst affected, with GDP declining 20 percent, paving the way for the emergence of Hitler, while French GDP fell by 16 percent. The UK was affected less, with a decline of 6 percent, though unemployment, already high in the 1920s at around 10 percent, rose to 20 percent. The slowdown was spread around the world by the impact of the Gold Standard (initially) and then increasingly by declining trade, protectionism, and weak business confidence.

Starting in 1933 the US enjoyed a rapid economic recovery, with GDP growing an average 9 percent per annum during 1933–7. However, output only recovered to 1929 levels in 1937 and the economy suffered a new downturn in 1937–8, though much more moderate. Other countries also recovered after 1933 but, as in the United States, it took some time to regain earlier peaks and unemployment remained relatively high for several years. Some commentators believe that it was only the Second World War and rearmament, creating massive new investment needs, that finally enabled the world to escape from the Depression.

EXPLAINING THE DEPRESSION

As we have seen, there was an interaction between monetary policy, asset prices, structural changes, and the business cycle. But in the voluminous literature on the Depression there are broadly three types of explanations.

BUSINESS CYCLE EXPLANATIONS

These approaches focus on the reasons for the spiraling decline in investment and consumer spending. According to this view, there was "overinvestment" in the 1920s and a natural pullback in the 1930s when the business cycle turned down. The explanations vary somewhat between those that emphasize shocks and policy mistakes and those that rely more on a natural cycle of investment. Several shocks have been documented. Exports were affected by the world slowdown, starting in 1930. US farm prices fell sharply, which hurt the incomes and therefore the spending of farmers, though of course improved the incomes of town dwellers. And this view would also give some weight to wealth and confidence effects arising from the stock market collapse and bank failures. The policy mistakes include the protectionist moves and the tightening of monetary policy in late 1931 in response to the British move off the Gold Standard. One very unhelpful policy often cited was the Smoot–Hawley tariff bill of 1930, a protectionist measure that rapidly brought retaliation from other countries and helped to precipitate the sterling crisis, which in turn led to the US tightening of monetary policy.

These cyclical explanations emphasize the variability of investment. High investment in the 1920s created jobs and boosted income and spending in general, which at first helped to supply the purchasing power for the new goods produced. But at some point, as the new capacity increasingly came on stream, there was less need for new investment. When investment spending slowed, employment and incomes fell, beginning a cumulative downturn in incomes and spending. In 2000–2 US investment spending also slumped and pessimists on the prospects for economic recovery expected it to stay low. However, in 2003–4 investment made a strong recovery. Time will tell whether this is sustained.

MONETARY INTERPRETATIONS

Monetary policy had responded well to the slowdown in late 1929–30, but then became too restrictive in late 1931–2. There are a number of different strands here, some related to gold and some to the money stock. In essence, the key argument (following Friedman and Schwartz) is that GDP declined because of a fall in nominal money supply, which the Fed failed to counter with expansionary policy.[7]

Opponents of this view argue that the fall in money supply was a result (not a cause) of reduced economic activity. They would agree that the Fed should have tried harder to offset it, particularly in 1931–2 when policy was actually restrictive, but question whether the Fed can in fact control the money supply anyway. In 2000–3 money growth continued in the 6–10 percent per annum range, somewhat stronger than for much of the 1990s.

FINANCIAL EXPLANATIONS

This approach focuses on the impact of the bank failures themselves.[8] Overall about 40 percent of the banks in existence in 1929 disappeared over the following four years, mostly through closures (though some reopened later) and amalgamations. The suspended banks accounted for about 15 percent of total deposits in the system and total deposits lost amounted to about 2 percent of GDP (in total, so about ½ percent of GDP per annum). According to this view, the weakened banking system was unable or unwilling to lend, even to creditworthy borrowers, so credit declined and new investment opportunities were not taken up. One interpretation of this unwillingness to lend is that banks suddenly viewed the world much more cautiously, given the wave of losses and bankruptcies around them. They simply doubted their own ability to judge whether businesses or projects were viable, given falling asset prices and the huge uncertainty in the economy, and they therefore played safe. In 2000–4 banks were very strong, reporting limited problems with losses. Profits were boosted by the gap between low short-term rates and higher long-term rates, as well as the burgeoning of housing finance.

Seventy years on from the event, scholars are still divided as to which of these three broad approaches best describes the causes of the Depression. The argument is crucial because of the policy implications for countries now in a low- or zero-inflation world. Broadly speaking, there is agreement that governments and central banks can avoid one important causal factor, the collapse of the banking system. And they should try to avoid the second, weak money growth, though how to do this and indeed whether it is possible is a cause of debate, notably in the case of Japan, as we shall see later. Governments can also avoid protectionism. But in my view all three approaches underplay the importance of the bubble in asset prices and the vulnerability that it creates.

THE ROLE OF ASSET PRICES

Let's step back a moment and look at the story through the prism of asset price developments. First of all, the rise in the market in the 1920s played a major role in promoting the economic boom. High levels of investment, strong consumption growth, and the overall euphoria of the period were clearly linked to the bubble in the stock market, just as we saw more recently in the 1990s. An earlier pricing of the stock market bubble would thus not only have reduced the losses suffered later, but would have reduced the gains and therefore perhaps have restrained the economic boom.

The Crash of 1929 broke the euphoria of the Roaring 20s, but in itself did not cause the Depression. In early 1930 the Dow Jones index rallied back to almost 300, about the level of late 1928 or early 1929. But starting in May 1930 it began a new decline and by the end of 1930 it was less than half the peak 1929 level (before the Fed mistakenly tightened credit again); in 1931–2 it declined further, to the eventual low of 90 percent down from the 1929 high. At this point the psychology of a collapsing bubble may have played an important role, as stockholders simply turned away from stocks altogether after so much disappointment.

Peak-to-trough comparisons can exaggerate the impact of market declines, of course. Few people actually buy at the top or count the top as their actual wealth level, while the trough lasts only a short while, by definition. But the Dow Jones index spent about three years at 200 or above (with the peak at over 350) between 1928 and the end of 1930. From late 1931 onward, when the Depression really took hold, it was at or below 100 (half that level) and remained there until 1935. Most investors must therefore have felt that they had lost well over half their stock market wealth, while many lost much more, especially those who had bought stocks on margin.

Property prices are less well documented for this period, but they declined sharply too. Home prices fell an estimated 30 percent during the period and commercial property prices fell as well.[9] The value of small farms collapsed, sparking the great migrations described so poignantly in John Steinbeck's novel, *The Grapes of Wrath*. Although the percentage declines in property prices were less than for stocks, the impact may have been as great or even greater, working through collateral losses and the effects on banks.

In summary, while it is certainly right to say that the 1929 Crash did not cause the Depression, the subsequent massive further decline in stocks and property, together with the associated effect on banks through defaults on mortgages, surely played a role. And the extent of these falls would likely have been far less if the increases in the late 1920s had been less dramatic. I would not deny that the largest single reason for the Depression was the unfortunate tightening of monetary policy in 1931 due to the adherence to the Gold Standard. But I think the case can be argued that it was the state of the cycle combined with the path of asset prices that made this tightening so disastrous. A bubble renders the economy highly vulnerable to shocks or policy mistakes.

In the next chapter we turn to the second-largest bubble of the twentieth century, Japan in the 1980s. While Japan avoided a full-scale depression after its bubble burst, economic growth has been dismal until very recently. Moreover, there is a shocking contrast between the confident, world-beating Japan of the 1980s, admired and feared by manufacturers around the world, and the basket case of the 1990s. Whereas $1,000 invested in the US stock market in 1990 would be worth $5,000 today (with the S&P index at 1,100), the same investment in Japan would be worth only just over $500.

3 JAPAN AND THE SPECTER OF DEFLATION

After the devastating experience of the 1930s, the next several decades saw comparatively few major asset price bubbles. By the 1970s bubbles and depressions were viewed as largely ancient history and the dominant worries in the world economy were sky-high oil prices and inflation. This complacency was rudely shattered by the experience of Japan. Not only did Japan suffer a massive bubble and then a severe bust that held back economic growth for more than a decade, but the ugly specter of deflation, not seen since the 1930s, reemerged. Japan's story illustrates how bubbles and deflation can interact. A collapsed bubble can easily lead to deflation because of the danger of a sharp economic downturn. And then deflation itself makes the downturn more severe and the task of restoring economic growth much more difficult.

In the late 1980s Japan's stock and property markets went to extraordinary valuations. The stock market reached price–earnings multiples of 60 times earnings and accounted for 45 percent of world stocks by total value, even though Japan produced only about 10 percent of world GDP. Property price moves were even more extreme, with rental yields becoming negligible and values per square meter in central Tokyo reaching astonishing heights. The government's land price index for six big cities tripled between 1985 and 1990 (see Chart 3.1).

Rising stock prices were closely linked to rising property prices. Many companies owned property and the value of that property was rising at an exponential rate. So, quite logically, those companies' stocks rose to reflect that value. Taking the example in Chapter 1, it was as though WhizzPizza owned all its restaurant properties and, because retail properties were soaring in value, its own stock was rising too, even

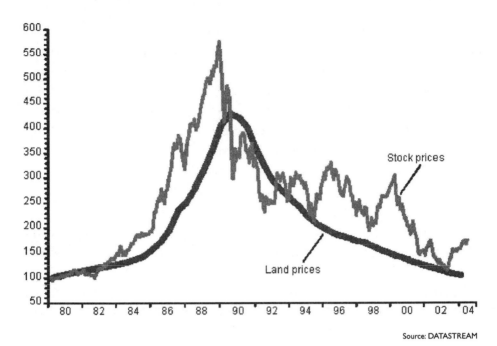

Source: DATASTREAM

Chart 3.1
Japan's bubble

without selling a single extra pizza. For the individual company this process might make sense because it could sell its properties and lease them back, but for the market as a whole it did not add up.

The drivers for Japan's bubble were, as usual, optimism and liquidity. Optimism was driven by a positive view of the economy, with strong growth and low inflation. But it went further than that. In the late 1980s Japan had come to be seen as the most successful economy in the world. Books were published forecasting that it was soon going to be number one, taking economic leadership from the United States. Management manuals were full of Japanese techniques such as total quality control, just-in-time inventories, and how to motivate the workforce. While most foreign companies balked at the idea of a company song, few people had any doubt that, in manufacturing at least, the Japanese were the ones to beat.

Economic growth averaged 5.4 percent per annum from 1987–90, after a dip to 3.1 percent in 1986. Productivity growth grew a rapid 4.6 percent per annum over the same period, helping to control inflation.

Profits grew at an average 8 percent per annum during the whole decade of the 1980s, well ahead of inflation, and there seemed to be no reason why rapid growth could not continue. Meanwhile, business investment rose from 18 percent of GDP in 1985 to 25 percent in 1990.

The liquidity bubble began with the agreement by the Japanese authorities to boost economic growth after the world slowdown of 1986. The US faced a weak dollar and felt that it was time for Germany and Japan to become the locomotives of growth by stimulating domestic spending. While Germany largely demurred, Japan responded positively to this request. The Bank of Japan (BOJ) cut the Official Discount Rate from 5 percent in 1985 to 2.5 percent in 1987 and kept it there until 1989. Money supply (measured by M2+CDs, Japan's main measure[1]) accelerated to over 10 percent per annum during 1987–90, well ahead of inflation of around 3 percent per annum. There is a close parallel here with the US decision in 1925 to cut interest rates to help the UK maintain the pound on the Gold Standard.

Japan's booming markets were widely seen as a bubble outside Japan, though not generally within the country. Many outside observers were shocked in 1987 when the US stock market crashed by 30 percent in October, but the Japanese market, almost alone in the world, hardly reacted. This immunity cheered Japanese investors and the market went on to attain new heights over the following two years. Investors justified the levels of the stock and property market in terms of expectations of continued profit gains for stocks and excess demand for space for property. On the property side, Japan had very restrictive land-use laws and the earthquake risk tended to limit the introduction of tall buildings.

The turnaround in 1990–91 can be traced to a tightening of monetary policy and a slowdown in business investment. The discount rate was hiked to 6 percent in 1990 and only reduced gradually after that, despite a sharp economic slowdown. The rise in interest rates was explicitly aimed at reducing land prices, not just at combating inflation, which in fact was not much of a problem. The fall in investment was partly a response to the rise in interest rates and reduced expectations for economic growth. But it also reflected the massive over-investment in capacity that had taken place. The pattern closely resembled the US experience in the 1930s, described in Chapter 2.

From the peak at the very end of 1989 stock prices fell 46 percent in nine months and remained weak throughout the 1990s, dipping to new lows in 2003, down a total of 75 percent from 13 years earlier. Land prices started a long slide that saw the six big city index give up all of its gains from 1985–90 by 2001 and prices in 2003–4 only now seem to be bottoming. Average GDP growth from 1991–2003 was only 1 percent per annum, with productivity growth averaging zero. The ratio of private business investment to GDP fell from its peak of 21 percent in 1990 to 15 percent in 2003, though this remained relatively high by world standards.

The weak economy combined with lower asset prices, particularly property prices, brought huge amounts of nonperforming loans, rendering the financial sector close to bankruptcy. Bad loans were privately estimated to be some 20–25 percent of GDP in 2001. Banks also faced the problem that part of their capital base (according to a special provision for Japan in the Basle capital arrangements[2]) is made up of gains on stockholdings. At the end of the 1980s these were substantial and gave banks a major cushion. After the stock market collapse, a large part of these gains disappeared. Bank lending grew slowly until 1997 but then loans outstanding started to fall, despite continuing positive money supply growth. Banks wanted to reduce their loans because of their weak capital base, while companies were trying to reduce their borrowings. These borrowings made sense when asset prices were high, but now left companies highly exposed.

In many ways the surprise is that Japan's economy has not performed even worse. The collapse in asset prices resembled the US experience in the 1930s but, although Japan has suffered a series of moderate recessions with short-lived recoveries, there has been no depression. Unemployment rose, but to nothing like the levels seen in the US in the 1930s. While policy could not prevent economic weakness, it did avoid a depression. Interest rates were cut, starting in 1991, and eventually were brought all the way down to zero. It is true that real short-term interest rates were never reduced below zero, as they could have been before deflation set in. But the BOJ at least did not deliver a major "shock" to the economy comparable to the Fed's tightening in 1931. Meanwhile fiscal policy has been highly stimulatory, more so than in the US in the 1930s. The government allowed the budget to swing from a surplus of 2.9 percent of GDP in 1990 to a deficit of 7 percent by 1999. Some of this swing represented a conscious Keynesian-style stimulus, concentrated on construction projects, but most was caused by leaving spending and tax levels in place in the face of slower economic growth.

A key difference to the US experience in the 1930s is that the Japanese government underwrote the banking system and did not allow depositors to lose money. So there were no bank runs and few closures. As a result, although money and credit growth has been weak, it has not collapsed as it did in the US in the 1930s. Moreover, confidence has held up better. Part of the reason for this may be that Japanese companies continued to invest, albeit at lower rates. And a key factor for Japan, in contrast to the US in the 1930s, is that the world economy was much stronger overall in the 1990s than in the 1930s, supporting strong Japanese export growth.

Another reason Japan avoided a full depression may be that the effect of the fall in asset prices on household wealth was not as great as might be expected. Net wealth peaked at 947 percent of incomes in 1990 and fell to 757 percent by 1995, where it stabilized.[3] But this is still high compared to other countries. The UK only reached 747 percent at the peak in 2000. Stockholdings in Japan were not a large part of household wealth even at the market high in 1989 and the losses were easily replenished by the high savings rate. Lower house prices hurt, though probably less than in other countries because of the tendency to regard houses as a long-term family investment. Moreover, falling interest rates helped substantially with mortgage costs. As a result, in recent years Japan's household savings rate has trended down from its prior very high levels, supporting consumer spending growth. The effect of the asset bust seems to have worked in Japan primarily through its impact on business confidence and on bank loans.

JAPAN AND DEFLATION

Between the 1950s and the mid-1990s deflation—falling consumer prices—was virtually unknown anywhere. The world's attention was focused entirely on battling rising prices, inflation, which had become the number one economic problem. But by the late 1990s the battle against inflation had been won and deflation had emerged in several countries in Asia, including Japan.

Central banks and economists are broadly agreed that the ideal behavior of the price level is for a small annual inflation rate in the range of 1–3 percent per annum, rather than a zero rate. One reason for this is the belief that inflation indices overstate inflation because quality improvements are not fully recognized by the statisticians. In the US the statistical approach was changed in the 1990s to try to reduce this problem, but many economists argue that inflation is still overstated.

The main reason, though, is that central banks are frightened of deflation. If they aim for zero inflation it would be easy to undershoot and create a falling price level. By aiming for a small positive rate of inflation, they leave themselves a slight cushion, so that in a mild slowdown or recession the rate of inflation may dip to zero or even just below, but deflation does not really take hold.

Deflation is a new and troubling threat for all of us brought up in an era of continuous inflation. Almost nobody alive today, even the venerable Mr. Greenspan, was an active market participant or policy maker in the 1930s, the last time the US and UK suffered deflation. Yet during the nineteenth century and right up to the 1930s, deflation was common, indeed even normal, while inflation was usually only seen at the height of economic booms and in wartime.

Though in the US and UK deflation is still only a hypothetical possibility, in Japan it has become a reality. In the early 1990s, with the bubble deflating rapidly but consumer price inflation still positive, the Japanese authorities struggled to achieve a sustained economic recovery. Each of a series of short-lived upswings was soon ended by a new downturn. The combination of falling asset prices, debt deflation, and a broken banking system made the economy highly vulnerable to each new shock that came along, whether the Asian crisis in 1997 or the world slowdown in 2001. In this weak environment inflation gradually dropped to zero and then deflation set in, starting in 1995. By 2004 Japan's price level had fallen a cumulative 10 percent and, despite a new upswing, expectations were for deflation to continue for at least another year.

The Bank of Japan reacted slowly when deflation first emerged. It cut interest rates to zero but did little more, to begin with. One reason was its firm belief that the economy needed major reforms, not merely monetary stimulus. In 2000 it even raised interest rates in an attempt to "normalize" interest costs and force companies to restructure. And in 1999–2000 it made an explicit attempt to link the introduction of vigorous antideflation measures to more rapid government reforms—a sort of "we will if you will" approach. The result was a standoff between the central bank and the government. Eventually there was a change in government and Prime Minister Koizumi accelerated the pace of government reform, but the delay certainly hurt the economy.

The second reason for caution was that the BOJ was terrified of being so successful at ending deflation that it created inflation. In the absence of real reforms, it feared that "printing money" would create high inflation or even hyperinflation (conventionally defined as inflation over 60 percent per annum) without stimulating the economy.

In 2001–3 the BOJ progressively accelerated its monetary stimulus. Partly as a result, but helped also by the strength of the Chinese economy together with a pickup in the US and Europe, the Japanese economy is showing renewed growth. There are also hopes that the stock market has finally seen a bottom, and perhaps land prices too. But deflation is continuing and the trend rate of economic growth, reckoned to be still only 1.5 percent, remains rather low. Meanwhile, further falls in the price level will continue to hold back asset prices and increase the real burden of debt. Also, one of the key legacies of the bubble is the large government debt, now about 160 percent of GDP. While this does not threaten an immediate crisis, it needs to be stabilized by reducing the budget deficit. So overall, while the outlook is brighter than for a long time, it is still too early to be sure that the impact of the bubble has finally been left behind.

A WORLD OF DEFLATION?

I am using the word deflation simply to mean the opposite of inflation; that is, a fall in consumer prices. It is also sometimes used to indicate a slump in the economy and a big fall in asset prices. But a decline in consumer prices does not have to involve a slump. During the late nineteenth century the US economy enjoyed a prolonged period of strong economic growth as it caught up with Britain, yet the price level gradually declined from the highs reached in the Civil War and in 1900 was about a third lower than in 1865.[4] There were years of slower growth and asset price decline, and these were often associated with a faster rate of deflation, but they were cyclical episodes rather than persistent trends. In recent years China has experienced periods of falling prices too, but growth has been solid.

So far only Japan, China, and Hong Kong have suffered more than a year or two of deflation, but we cannot rule out that it could become more widespread. Often what happens in this kind of long-run deflationary environment is that wage rates remain broadly stable, while the price level falls by the rate of productivity growth. So people gradually become better off over time as the costs of their purchases fall, rather than because they receive wage rises. The rate of deflation is usually about 1–2 percent per annum in this case. However, in particularly weak periods of the economic cycle, or during a serious slump, the price level can fall quite rapidly and this is often associated with falling asset prices at the same time. During the Depression the US price level fell by 25 percent between 1929 and 1933.

Barring a major slump, wage rates tend to put a limit on the extent of deflation because of strong resistance to cuts in wages. Nobody likes wage cuts even if the price level is falling too, because a wage cut brings an immediate loss. Contrast this with a wage rise. If prices are rising by, say, 2 percent per annum and workers receive a wage increase of 2 percent per annum, they are no better off over the course of the whole year but they are better off immediately after the pay rise, so of course they are happy with that. The same overall result would be achieved if both prices and wages were falling by 2 percent per annum, but at the moment of the wage cut the workers would immediately feel worse off. Workers often bitterly resist wage cuts unless times are really hard and they feel they have no choice.

Nevertheless, wage cuts are far from unknown. In Japan and Hong Kong wages have been falling because of cuts in bonuses, a significant part of compensation for many people, often explicitly paid as a

"thirteenth month's" salary. But wage cuts have also been directly implemented in some sectors, including the Hong Kong government itself.
And wages can also drift down when companies take on new employees at lower wage rates or through cutting back on benefits, for example health care or pension rights. It is possible too that deflation
encourages companies to push their employees to work harder or
longer, since they cannot simply raise prices to boost profits.

WHY DEFLATION MAKES BUBBLES MORE DANGEROUS

In a world of deflation, bubbles are much more risky affairs. Once the
bubble bursts, the subsequent fall in asset prices is likely to be much
larger than in a world of inflation. Whereas an ongoing positive inflation rate tends to underpin nominal values, a falling general price level
can make the fall in asset prices even worse. Japan's stock and land
prices were falling throughout the 1990s toward the floor, but from
1995, when deflation set in, the floor was moving downward too! If
inflation had remained positive, asset prices would have reached cheap
values much earlier.

This substantially increases the chance of "debt deflation," perhaps
the most feared phenomenon in economics because of its devastating
impact on both the economy itself and on the banking system. In a
debt deflation, asset prices start falling and investors begin to panic
because they have financed the assets with borrowings. Some sell
quickly to escape being under water on their debt. Others wait but
then, starting to worry that prices will fall still further, try to sell as
well, anxious to pay off their debts even at a loss. A few will be unable
to service their debts and will face foreclosure by the bank, which in
turn will try to sell the asset. But all this selling of assets of course
drives prices still lower, so that asset prices and the economy can enter
a vicious downward spiral.

Often people are forced to sell assets indiscriminately to meet debt
payments, and sometimes they will sell their better assets because they
are the only ones that can be sold quickly. Markets tend to break down

during severe busts so that assets like property or small businesses, which are not very liquid even at the best of times, can become almost unsalable at any price. Meanwhile banks may panic too. Normally a great deal of bank lending is linked to asset values, whether it is lending to small businesses through second mortgages on the entrepreneur's house or lending to investment banks against their securities' portfolio. During an asset price deflation, none of this can be relied on and banks tend to rush to call in their existing loans and be very cautious about new ones.[5]

This process of asset price deflation last occurred in the US in 1932–3, but as already mentioned such episodes were relatively common in the nineteenth century. They often resulted in runs on banks too, as people questioned whether particular institutions, or even the system as a whole, were sound. Central banks know how to prevent this now, through a combination of providing unlimited liquidity if necessary and also through the government guaranteeing bank deposits. While such measures can contain a panic, they cannot necessarily stop the steady selling of assets as people try to avoid further losses or escape their debts. During the inflationary period in the second half of the twentieth century, debt deflation was largely unknown. Even if asset prices fell sharply in real terms, rising general prices put a floor on the decline in nominal terms and so rescued debtors. But with inflation now very low, and especially if deflation sets in, we are much more at risk of debt deflation.

Japan has been going through debt deflation, though in a very slow, drawn-out manner and without any panic. Overall credit to the private sector has fallen by 17 percent since 1998, with companies concentrating on improving profits and cash flow rather than spending. But, partly because interest rates have been so low and partly because banks have been underpinned by the government, there has not been a panic. On the other hand, the very slow nature of the adjustment has prevented a rapid recovery.

Historically countries usually emerged from the vicious downward spiral of debt deflations only when asset prices had fallen substantially in real terms (i.e., further than consumer prices) and many debts had been written off. Then, usually after some time had elapsed or with the benefit of new investment opportunities arising from new technologies, the economy moved off again. But this is a very painful process and usually means a period of high unemployment and wage declines.

It is also a trauma for investors. Only cash and government bonds are completely safe in this environment and even then only if the government itself is sound. If there is a danger of a government default, these assets are unreliable too since the bonds could become worthless and, in the event of a banking crisis, the government would not be able to bail out the banks. Gold, the asset of last resort, often performs well in a time of deflation.

DEFLATION AND MONETARY POLICY

A further problem arising from deflation is that central banks cannot cut interest rates lower than zero. In an economic downturn the central bank normally cuts interest rates to stimulate the economy. This works through several mechanisms, but one of the most important is by boosting asset prices. Cuts in interest rates can also be used by the central bank to react to sudden crashes in asset prices. For example, the 1987 stock market crash, when stocks fell over 30 percent in two days in the US, UK, and most other countries, was met by cuts in interest rates in the following days and weeks. This helped to allow the markets to regain their October peaks within a year or so. It also gave investors some comfort that the central banks, at least to a degree, were on their side. This was sometimes referred to as the "Greenspan put," because it seemed to offer downside protection to investors in rather the same way as a put option. However, for Japan, the emergence of deflation in 1995 meant that interest rates lost traction once they hit zero (in 1999). And with the rate of deflation accelerating to around 2 percent per annum by the end of the decade, real interest rates actually rose at this point.

Asset prices are bolstered by cuts in short-term interest rates through several related mechanisms. First, rate cuts lower the yield on holding cash versus the yield from assets, whether it is the interest rate on bonds, the dividend from stocks, or the rental yield on property. Investors often respond by "reaching for yield," which means moving out of cash into bonds and stocks. Obviously this does depend on investors having positive expectations for asset prices. If they think that asset prices could fall, they will just hold on to cash even at low yields.

Secondly, lower cash rates may encourage people to borrow more, to buy assets. Given the yield available on assets, a lower borrowing cost can improve the attractiveness of a portfolio of assets, financed with borrowings. Clearly this will depend on expectations for asset prices, but also on the length of time that investors think interest rates will stay low.

Thirdly, in times of inflation cuts in interest rates can make *real* rates negative, which makes borrowing to buy assets especially attractive. For example, if the real interest rate is minus 5 percent, investors know that it is worth borrowing to buy an asset even if the asset price is expected to be stable in real terms. Investors also know that negative real interest rates are likely to stimulate the real economy by encouraging companies to increase investment and consumers to buy cars and so on. So the chances are that the economy will strengthen, making asset price falls less likely.

All these mechanisms have worked well for central banks during the last few decades of high inflation. But now translate this into a world of deflation, with the price level falling by perhaps 1–2 percent a year. Provided that the economy is growing reasonably well, it can probably live with short-term interest rates of 0–2 percent, giving a 2–3 percent level of real rates (a fairly normal range historically). However, if the economy slows suddenly, rates can fall only a little and real rates will inevitably remain positive. Indeed, the slowing economy may lead to a faster deflation (e.g., minus 2–4 percent annually), so that it may be hard to reduce real rates at all. Suddenly, in stark contrast to the economic history of the last 40 years, the central banks will have lost control.

POLICY MEASURES TO AVOID DEFLATION

So what are the policy measures that a central bank or government can take, if deflation threatens or is already underway?[6] First, short-term interest rates can be cut quickly, all the way to zero. One of the lessons of the Japanese experience is that it is worth being very aggressive in

doing this, if inflation is not at high levels, because that way the economy can be restarted more rapidly and inflation will not fall so far.
Much more rapid interest rate cuts in the first half of the 1990s in Japan
could have generated a negative real rate, something the BOJ never
managed.

Secondly, the central bank can push cash (or technically "reserves")
into the banking system. However, Japan has tried this in recent years
with limited success, because there is still no desire to borrow or lend.
The banking system already has too much bad debt and confidence in
the future is just too weak. As a result, money supply growth has
remained slow while lending to the economy has fallen.

The third possibility is to devalue the currency. This has the effect
of boosting economic growth through higher exports and lower
imports, but also directly increases the price level as foreign goods
become more expensive. A higher general price level also tends to support asset prices (measured in local currency, of course). But in a floating exchange rate environment countries cannot devalue at will
because the markets decide the exchange rate. And cutting interest
rates to send the currency lower is not possible if they are already at
zero. So the options open to governments are to try to talk the currency down, which is likely to be of limited effect, or to intervene
actively in the foreign exchange market to buy foreign currency for
home currency.

While Japan has tried to engineer a weaker yen, it has had only limited success despite massive purchases of US dollars in 2003–4, because
it has a large current account surplus. Meanwhile, individual countries
in Europe cannot devalue either if they have joined the Eurozone. The
UK is in a relatively good position here, outside the euro, since the
pound could fall if deflation ever took hold. Similarly, Australia has a
flexible currency that could adjust downward if necessary, as it did during the Asian crisis. Countries with a free-floating exchange rate and relatively small size are the most likely to be able to use devaluation
successfully.

The fourth policy for fighting deflation is to promise to hold
short-term interest rates low for an extended period, which should
have the effect of bringing yields on shorter-dated bonds—for exam-

ple up to two or three years or perhaps longer—down too. The US used this approach in 2003 in various statements, as did the Bank of Japan.

The fifth possible approach is for the central bank to buy assets from the private sector.[7] This has the effect of putting money directly into people's hands and driving down yields on these assets. The Bank of Japan has been buying government bonds for several years, driving 10-year yields below 1 percent at times, and has also purchased small amounts of stocks.

The final approach is for the government to expand spending or cut taxes, financed with bonds that are directly purchased by the central bank. A similar effect is obtained if the bonds are purchased by ordinary banks, provided that these banks are also supplied with ample reserves from the central bank. This is, in essence, fiscal spending financed by printing money. It would work, even if the central bank just started to buy bonds to finance an existing deficit, which previously had been financed by private-sector purchases of bonds. It would work better still if the government announced new tax cuts or spending plans, to be financed by the central bank.

With full use of these measures there is little doubt that it is possible to end deflation. And the recent signs are that, since about 2002 when Japan finally embraced them wholeheartedly, they are having some success. But there is a problem. It is very difficult for central banks to know how much money to put into the banking system or how many bonds to buy and they may be nervous about overdoing it, creating inflation down the road. Japan was forced to abandon its earlier, cautious approach but, assuming that the economy continues to recover, it will need to withdraw the stimulus gradually in coming years.

In the aftermath of the US 1990s stock market bubble, the authorities clearly had in mind the Japanese experience as well as the history of the 1930s. For the US in 2001, deflation seemed far away, with core inflation (excluding food and energy) still at 1.8 percent. But inflation dropped sharply in 2002 and by 2003 was below 1 percent and still falling. Suddenly, with the economic recovery only lackluster, deflation began to seem like a real possibility. The US authorities made it clear that they would be very proactive in avoiding deflation if possible and also in dealing with it if necessary. The next chapter brings our story up to date as we look at the aftermath of the 1990s bubble.

4 THE GREENSPAN BUBBLE AND REFLATION

Few doubt that it would have been better if the 1990s stock bubble had not occurred. But in Chairman Greenspan's view, restraining the market in the 1990s would have been difficult, and deliberately pricking the bubble would have been dangerous. His critics counter that a tighter monetary policy in 1997–9 could have helped limit the bubble and, moreover, that Greenspan erred in becoming a cheerleader for stocks. During 1997–2000 he abandoned earlier talk of "irrational exuberance," instead extolling the virtues of the "new economy" and suggesting that market valuations should not be questioned.

When the bubble burst in 2001 Greenspan switched quickly to dealing with the consequences. And so far at least, the demise of the 1990s stock market bubble has been far less damaging than either the US 1930s depression or Japan's recent experience. The US recession in 2001 proved comparatively mild and unemployment rose by a modest 2.5 percentage points. Even the decline in the market was not as extreme as in the two earlier experiences, at least if we take the broader US indices. At the trough in 2002 the US S&P 500 index was down just under 50 percent from its 2000 peak, compared with falls of 80–90 percent in 1930s America and 1990s Japan.

There are some who believe that the bust is not yet over. They expect that the 2003–4 upswing will quickly come to grief, ushering in a new bear market and a renewed economic downturn. Many cite investor psychology, arguing that, when a bubble bursts and the bubble psychology changes, it is unnatural for stocks to stop falling before they become very cheap. This was certainly true of the two largest US bear markets of the twentieth century, the 1930s and the 1970s, where price–earnings ratios bottomed at below 10, in contrast to the trough around 15 in 2002 (based on operating earnings). But these past bear markets also coincided with severe economic problems, depression with deflation in the 1930s and severe recession with inflation in the 1970s. Now, with the economy and profits growing and inflation moderately positive, there would seem to be no reason for investors to become that pessimistic.

In my view, while the ultra-bearish scenario cannot be completely ruled out, it looks unlikely to develop in the immediate future for two reasons. One is that, in contrast to the experience of the 1920s and Japan in the 1980s, the 1990s bubble was focused on stocks. Neither commercial nor residential property participated to any great extent. Both had suffered in the early 1990s during the economic downturn and this probably contributed to a cautious approach by investors. Commercial property prices were soft in the US in 2000–2, with occupancy rates down somewhat and rents declining. But the weakness was only modest and there were very few cases of distress. The banking system was barely affected.

Meanwhile, residential prices rose during the collapse of the stock bubble, in response to the very rapid cuts in interest rates. While unemployment moved up and consumer confidence was as weak as in the early 1990s, people still retained sufficient confidence to buy houses. As a result consumers' overall wealth level, though dented by the collapse in the stock market, remained at historically high levels. And this was crucial to the relatively mild nature of the economic slowdown. The short-lived 2001 recession was entirely due to action by US companies to cut inventory and scale back fixed investments, particularly in computer software. Consumer spending sailed through, growing more slowly than in the boom years but still expanding. And car sales remained strong.

The second reason it is different this time is the policy response. In 1931, when policy was tightened to protect the Gold Standard, the rise in interest rates hit the economy when it was deeply vulnerable and led to the Depression. Trying to maintain fixed currency arrangements is a frequent and, sadly, oft-repeated mistake in monetary history. The same error was made by the Hong Kong government in 1997–9, when it clung obstinately to the Hong Kong dollar currency peg (to the US dollar) despite a severe recession and falling asset prices. As a result stock and property prices fell even further and Hong Kong suffered a miserable few years. In the early 1990s Japan's mistake was to move too slowly and too cautiously.

In 2001–3 the Fed did not have any currency arrangements to hold to. Nor was it worried about consumer price inflation. And it was determined to avoid the mistakes of the past. It did have some concerns over inflation in the late 1990s but, once the recession began in 2001, attention shifted to the risk of deflation. Meanwhile, President Bush had been elected partly on the promise of tax cuts. As originally conceived, these cuts were in the Reagan "supply side" tradition, designed to stimulate enterprise and growth. But by early 2001, when George Bush took office, the case for tax cuts shifted to the need to kick-start the economy. In the end the total fiscal stimulus from the US government during 2001–3 amounted to over 3 percent of GDP, the largest in history.

For a while it looked as though this massive combined stimulus still might not be enough. Though the dollar was not locked into any exchange rate system, it remained persistently high in 2001, limiting any help from this source. Normally such a large monetary loosening works partly through a weaker currency, but the dollar responded only slowly, not easing back until 2002–3. Meanwhile, stocks trended down, reaching a low in October 2002, rebounding a little and then retesting the low in early 2003. The terrorist attacks of September 11th, 2001 sent a shock wave around the world, seeming to threaten the prospects of recovery too. The Fed responded to this new shock with more interest rate cuts and, starting in 2002, the economy began a sluggish recovery. But growth was held back in early 2003 by fears over the Iraq war and high oil prices and there were serious doubts about its sustainability.

At the time of writing (July 2004), most of these doubts have been put to rest. The economic upswing has gained broad-based strength and confidence has rebounded. There is always the possibility of shocks to the system, perhaps from renewed instability in the Middle East, but barring this, the economy seems set to continue to grow reasonably solidly at least into 2005. Forecasting is a hazardous business of course but, at least for a while, the recovery seems to be on firm ground. The fiscal stimulus will wane as the effects of the tax cuts wear off, but interest rates are likely to be raised only gradually, at least at first, so determined is the Fed to avoid deflation, thus the monetary stance will remain supportive for a while.

The stock market has recovered strongly too and is now at 75 percent of its peak 2000 level (for the S&P 500, the NASDAQ is still at less than half its peak). As already noted, there is no reason for the stock market to collapse again, provided that the recovery continues and the news remains good. But during the bubble years many plans were made based on the expectation that stocks would continue to rise from already high levels. Some people probably anticipated continued double-digit rises, which was always wildly ambitious.

However, many people thought they were being reasonable in projecting 8–10 percent gains on an ongoing basis, close to long-term averages. If stock markets had continued to rise at 8 percent per annum, from end 1999 levels, by 2005 they would have been 47 percent higher, implying an S&P 500 of 2,115 and a FTSE 100 of 8,400. These levels are now completely out of reach, with current market levels only at around half the expected level.

Some investors have already adjusted to lower levels. But many long-term investment plans are still in disarray, and nowhere is this more evident than with funded pensions. The difficulties with pensions are sometimes ignored because they are a long-term concern, not an immediate problem, for most people at least. But the truth is that the bubble and bust have thrown them into crisis and this has important implications for the economy.

PENSIONS IN CRISIS

Pensions are in crisis for two reasons. One is demographic, the combined effects of increasing longevity and the low birth rate in reducing the proportion of people working relative to the number in retirement. The other is the continuing aftershocks from the 1990s stock bubble. For state pensions, funded out of taxation, the demographic problem is the overwhelming issue. Will working people in the coming decades be willing to pay the taxes required to meet the pension promises that have been made? The answer is frequently no, which is why governments in continental Europe, where state pensions are dominant (and generous), have been desperately struggling to scale back the commitment. But for any sort of funded pension, whether a company scheme or a private pension, it is the bubble and bust in the stock market that form the main issue.

In an ideal world pensions should be unaffected by bubbles. Pensions are ultra-long-term financial contracts, with individuals or their employers paying in to an investment fund over several decades and then receiving payouts for, potentially, two or three decades after that. Pension managers should be able to invest for the long term and easily survive the odd bubble, maybe even make money out of riding it and then exiting at a timely moment. But it has not worked out like that in the last few years. What went wrong?

The basic problem is that companies took advantage of the bubble to enjoy "payment holidays" so that, instead of adding funds during the good times, they cut contributions. This was sometimes encouraged by governments, which frowned on "overfunding" pensions, since pension contributions are made out of pretax profits and therefore could be seen as a tax dodge. In the UK the problem was exacerbated by a government "raid" on pension schemes from 1998, which taxed the dividend income of pension schemes for the first time.

Payment holidays of course meant higher profits, which helped to keep down the reported price–earnings ratio on stocks and may have contributed to the inflation of the bubble. In the US, accounting regulations made it possible not only to skip payments but, by simply raising the expected return on existing pension funds, to report higher profits.[1] During the bubble years projections of double-digit investment returns were widespread, despite the fall in overall inflation that should have reduced them.

Today, following the collapse in stock markets, many defined-benefit schemes are seriously underfunded. In February 2004, after the rebound in the stock market, US companies were estimated to have an overall deficit of $350 billion.[2] UK companies face proportionately larger problems, with the deficit estimated at £100 billion at the end of 2003.[3]

Calculating the extent of underfunding depends on various assumptions, the most uncertain being future investment returns. During the bubble everybody took an optimistic view, from companies through to government regulators. Now many companies still want to take an optimistic view, so that they can at least spread out the extra payments they may need to make. Many US companies continue to assume investment returns in the 8–10 percent range. Such returns are not impossible, and indeed are more likely from today's lower stock market levels, but they may still be a stretch. Since yields on bond holdings will be well below 8–10 percent in today's markets, except on very high-risk securities, returns on stocks have to be assumed to be above 8–10 percent.

Meanwhile, there is growing pressure from accountants and regulators to take a conservative view of likely returns. Partly this reflects the reaction to the bubble, which has put new emphasis on conservative accounting. But from the government standpoint, there is also a concern that, if companies underfund their pension schemes and then go bankrupt, the government may end up having to bail out pensioners with taxpayers' money.

US corporate pensions are protected by an insurance scheme called the Pension Benefit Guarantee Corporation (PBGC). Set up 30 years ago, this insures basic pension provision for about 44 million Americans. However, at the end of 2003, despite having had 30 years to collect insurance premiums, it had a deficit of $11.2 billion. Moreover, the PBGC has warned that there are $85 billion in pension deficits in weak companies.[4] The US government has bowed to lobbying pressure and eased the accounting regulations on pension schemes to allow companies to carry these deficits for now. But unless markets rise strongly, the problem will not go away.

In the UK the government is setting up a similar institution to protect the more than 18,000 schemes still open. However, this will be a new burden on employers and there is a danger that responsible employers will end up subsidizing less responsible ones, though the government's proposals do suggest adjusting premiums for risk. But, in the absence of an existing scheme, an estimated 60,000 people have lost all or part of their pension in the last few years when their companies went bankrupt with underfunded schemes. The British government is proposing a special compensation scheme, but it offers only partial compensation.[5]

For the large number of companies that now face underfunded schemes, there are three ways out. They can put more money into the fund, they can somehow reduce the payouts, or they can hope that stock markets recover rapidly. Many are relying on a combination of all three. Most companies are increasing contributions. This represents a drag on profits and, in Britain at least, may also be slowing investment in expanding the company. The Confederation of British Industry has argued that an important reason for weak business investment in Britain in 2003–4 has been the need for companies to increase their pension contributions.[6] US investment has been more robust. A few companies have issued new debt to raise cash for their pension schemes, but that only makes sense if the pension managers can generate a higher return than the interest on debt.

Some companies are finding ways to reduce the payout. Generally speaking, pensions that have already been earned with service to date cannot be changed retrospectively. But the way the scheme works in future can be adjusted to make it less generous. Some companies are also finding ways to cut back on "fringe benefits," such as private health-care insurance. Ultimately though, most companies, as well as governments and regulators, are crossing their fingers and hoping that investment returns will prove good in coming years so that the problem will gradually fade.

But if stock markets underperform, many companies will face a continuing drag on profits and some weak companies with large pension schemes could go under as a result. The worst affected are in old industries, such as the auto and steel companies in the United States. In the worst-case scenario, where the stock market bears are right and stocks fall back to much lower levels, the problem could become enormous. Such an environment is most likely in the event of a new recession and it would undoubtedly make the downturn much worse.

Meanwhile defined-contribution schemes, where the employer and/or employee puts money into a scheme to be invested in the markets, as well as personal pension plans (such as 401K schemes in the US), are also worth much less than hoped in 2000. Many people planning to retire soon find that they have far less in the pension pot than they expected. Moreover, if they want to buy an annuity, rates are lower than a few years ago because of the general fall in interest rates. People face the choice of accepting a lower standard of living than they anticipated or working for longer.

In Britain a particular problem has emerged with a type of investment called an endowment mortgage. The idea sounded good in theory and these products were widely sold in the 1980s and early 1990s. Instead of taking out a normal repayment mortgage, where monthly payments include both interest and a partial repayment of principal, homeowners pay only interest on the mortgage loan but also pay into an investment fund (the endowment), which is projected to grow large enough to pay off the whole mortgage at maturity, usually after 25 years. Indeed, many were expected to pay large cash bonuses on top.

The trouble is that when these investments were initiated, interest rates were typically in the 7–12 percent range and it was reasonable to project overall investment returns of 10–15 percent or more. However, since then inflation and interest rates have come down and investment returns have been much lower. For a while the 1990s bubble concealed the problem because returns were so strong. But after the stock market collapse the deficits have been starkly revealed. An estimated 75 percent of endowments will fail to pay off the mortgages linked to them, so homeowners will need to come up with other savings or extend their mortgages. Many believe that the products were missold. Perhaps they were if people did not realize the investment risk involved, though endowment holders have not necessarily lost out overall as they have been paying much lower interest rates than originally expected. Still, as these products mature over the next 10 years or so, some homeowners are in for a nasty shock.

SAVINGS RATES TOO LOW

Despite the collapse of the stock market bubble, many people still have overoptimistic views of investment returns and their future wealth. This is perhaps best seen by looking at savings rates. In the US the savings

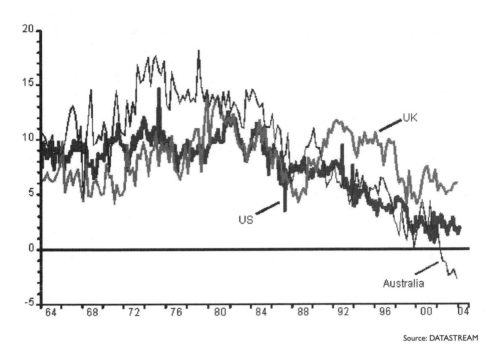

Source: DATASTREAM

Chart 4.1
Household savings rates

rate is at only about 2 percent of disposable income, low compared to past averages and also low in relation to the levels likely to be necessary for the long term. In Australia the savings rate has turned negative, indicating that high borrowing is overwhelming people's savings. The UK does not appear so extreme as the others (see Chart 4.1), though the rate is near cyclical lows.

It is not hard to understand the reason for depressed savings rates. After all, unemployment is relatively low, the economy is growing, house prices are rising strongly, and the stock market has bounced back from its 2002 lows. There is a natural tendency to save less. Moreover, the savings rate is calculated simply as the difference between income and spending so, when borrowing is strong, the rate is depressed. But if asset prices underperform in future and borrowing slows, savings rates will rise sharply and the economy will be weak as a result.

If the US rate rose to 8 percent in a hurry, a recession would be hard to avoid. The combined Greenspan–Bush stimulus in 2001–3 worked so well that, despite the recession and rise in unemployment, the savings rate rose only marginally. Achieving this a second time might not be so easy, particularly with so much less ammunition available for stimulus. The high US budget deficit is a particular cause for worry.

GOVERNMENT BUDGET DEFICITS TOO HIGH

The US deficit is expected to remain above 4 percent of GDP in 2005–6, in the absence of spending restraint or a rollback of the tax cuts. And on some projections it remains high right into the next decade. Official projections are somewhat disingenuous because they assume that the tax cuts will be discontinued in future years, the so-called sunset clauses. But the reality is that this will require a political decision and will be far from easy. If economic growth could remain at 4 percent or so for some years, the problem would diminish over time. But if growth should disappoint, the deficit would balloon to 5–6 percent or more, even without a new stimulus program.

Budget deficits in Europe have also moved higher since the bubble burst, hitting the 3–4 percent range in all the major countries. The UK bears the closest resemblance to the US, in that the budget moved from a surplus in the bubble years to a deficit now and was helped on its way by a deliberate government stimulus. Continental Europe never did manage surpluses in the boom times and its larger deficits mainly reflect the economic slowdown, with only a modest deliberate stimulus.

Of course, an economic downturn usually leaves government budgets in deficit and this is no bad thing. It has long been accepted that governments should allow the budget to swing into deficit in a recession to help provide an "automatic stabilizer" to the economy. Tax revenues naturally fall and unemployment benefits rise. However, the bubble made the fall in tax revenues worse this time, particularly in the US and UK. In the late 1990s the tax take was artificially boosted as revenues were collected from individuals cashing in on stock options and gains on shares, only to fall back more than usual in 2001–3.[7]

Budget deficits do not pose an immediate threat to the economy. Government debt ratios are modest in the US and Europe and there is no difficulty financing a deficit, even up to 5–6 percent of GDP for a sustained period, as Japan demonstrated in the 1990s. Japan's deficit averaged 7 percent between 1998 and 2004, despite the debt ratio climbing above 100 percent of GDP, much higher than in the US and Europe.

Nevertheless, budget deficits are widely recognized as problematic in the long run, for two main reasons. One is that if the government is borrowing so much, there is less available for the private sector. The result over time is usually higher interest rates because of the competition for funds, and this leads to lower business investment and slower economic growth.

Secondly, rising debt ratios do eventually matter. At some point, the debt has to be controlled. If not, eventually the government will have to pay more to borrow because people fear either a default or a bout of inflation (often the way governments effectively default). In Japan's case, if it can restore inflation to the 1–2 percent range in coming years, this will put government tax revenues on an upward track and help to pay the interest on debt issued in recent years at very low yields. But yields on new borrowing will rise too, probably back to the 3–5 percent range eventually. After a while, when cheap debt matures and has to be replaced with higher-yielding debt, the arithmetic will quickly become very difficult unless Japan can get the overall debt burden on a downward track.

While the debt ratios in the US and Europe are much lower than in Japan, the headline figures tend to understate governments' true liabilities, because pension promises and quickly rising health spending as the population ages are not fully accounted. These are a problem in the US and UK and even more so in continental Europe, where the population is aging rapidly.

Bringing down budget deficits is not only painful, it is also difficult if the economy is weak. Japan attempted to pull back its deficit in 1997 but, partly as a result, the economy slumped in 1998 and the government had to postpone budget adjustment. In 2004–5, the economic upswing seems to be more broadly based and the budget deficit is expected to come down, but Japan will need several years of strong private-sector growth to enable the budget deficit to be brought fully under control.

Governments everywhere will be hoping for a prolonged economic upswing to enable the deficits to come back down again, partly through natural effects and partly through gradual fiscal tightening. This suggests that interest rates will stay relatively low in the next few years. Central banks will need to offset the effects of fiscal tightening by normalizing interest rates only gradually.

INTEREST RATES TOO LOW

In 2002–3 short-term interest rates were cut to 1 percent in the US, 2 percent in the Eurozone, 3.5 percent in the UK, and 4.25 percent in Australia. In Japan they stayed at zero, where they had been since 2001. Yet over the long run, a neutral rate of interest would normally be expected to be 2–3 percent above inflation, or around 4–5 percent if central banks are hitting their inflation target of around 2 percent. Of course, with economies weak and inflation *below* target, low rates made perfect sense. And the strength of world economic growth in 2003–4 suggests that they are having the desired effect. But these levels are unsustainable and rates are likely to increase to more normal levels at some point.

In the past, US tightening episodes have often been disruptive to asset markets. Chairman Greenspan's first direct experience of this was with the October 1987 stock market crash; he had taken over the chairmanship in August, just weeks before. The Fed had begun to move rates up earlier in the year and bonds markets slumped in the early summer. But stocks surged upward between January and August, encouraged by the strong economy and rising profits. The sudden crash in October, which took the US market down 30 percent in two trading days, was a severe shock. The immediate worry was that a crash like this, so reminiscent of the 1929 crash, would lead to a 1930s-style depression. Of course it did not, partly because Greenspan quickly cut rates, but also because the bubble and crash constituted a very short-lived affair. At the end of 1987 stocks were pretty much back where they started the year. Still, this was Greenspan's first experience of the difficulties of managing monetary tightening, especially in the presence of a bubble.

Once it became apparent that the 1987 market crash had had little impact outside Wall Street and the economy was still strong, a new tightening program began. Rates peaked in early 1989, at which point the economy began to slow. But, despite steady reductions in rates later in 1989 and 1990, the economy slid into recession in late 1990. Part of the reason was Saddam Hussein's invasion of Kuwait, which sent oil prices sharply higher. But the data imply that the economy was already heading into recession, suggesting that policy was eased too slowly.[8]

The next time Greenspan was hauling on the tightening levers was in 1994 and this is perhaps the closest comparison with the current environment. By 1994 a gradual, "jobless" recovery was giving way to renewed economic vigor. Unemployment had started to come down rapidly and it was believed that interest rates needed to be normalized. Rates went down to 3 percent in the early 1990s recession, but since inflation was also about 3 percent, this is directly comparable to the situation 10 years later, with both interest rates and inflation at 1 percent.

The Fed began to tighten in early 1994 and took rates up 3 percent in little more than a year. Again, bonds crashed, with yields jumping by a similar amount. However, the stock market dipped only a touch and then marched sideways, ending the tightening period close to where it began. Other countries' markets performed in a similar way, except those in continental Europe, which did somewhat better as it emerged from recession.

The best hope is that we will see a similar outcome this time. Bond yields dipped to 3.1 percent in mid-2003 and spent much of the following year in the 3.5–4.5 percent range. But if short-term rates are rising in the direction of 3–4 percent or so, 10-year bond yields could head toward the 5–6 percent range. It would seem difficult for stocks to make a great deal of progress in this environment, though if the economy is strong profits will be rising, providing some support.

This brings us to the final legacy of the stock bubble, perhaps the most important of all. In pulling out all the stops to escape the aftermath of the stock market crash, the danger is that a new bubble has been created, in housing. Buoyancy in house prices has been key to Greenspan's strategy for escaping the full implications of the stock bust. And for some people property has taken the place of stocks and pensions as a vehicle for funding retirement. However, valuations in housing are now high in the US and elsewhere, in sharp contrast to 1994. It is to housing that we turn in Part II.

PART II

HOUSING:
THE NEXT CRASH?

5 THE WORLDWIDE BOOM

Home prices have risen strongly in many countries in recent years. For those already on the housing ladder and particularly those who bought in the mid to late 1990s, gains have been stunning, especially with the leverage provided by mortgages. Where prices have been especially rampant—Ireland, the UK, Australia, and Spain for example—house values have become the favorite topic of conversation at dinner parties and barbecues. Even in the US, where home price inflation has been more moderate, the pace has picked up recently and valuations are becoming high by historical standards. One serious downside is that first-time buyers are finding houses increasingly unaffordable. But the real danger is that we are watching the emergence of dangerous new bubbles.

In the eight years 1995–2003 prices rose by a cumulative 193 percent in Ireland, 146 percent in the UK, 122 percent in Spain, and 110 percent in the Netherlands and Australia; see Table 5.1. In the US the rise was a rather more modest 61 percent, though some areas, particularly on the coasts, saw greater activity. All these increases were well ahead of the increase in consumer prices of around 10–20 percent. The three major exceptions were Germany and Japan, still mired in falling prices, and Switzerland, where prices have been stagnant overall.

Rapid price inflation does not, in itself, point to a bubble. Prices were generally depressed in the mid-1990s, so some of the rise may be legitimate catch-up. But measures of valuation, patchy as they are for housing in contrast to stocks, suggest that prices have now become unusually high compared with historical levels, in relation to both earnings and rents. One 2003 analysis, comparing house prices in relation to earnings with the average ratio from 1975–2002, found prices overvalued by 60 percent in Spain, around 50 percent in Britain, Ireland, and the Netherlands, 28 percent in Australia, and 14 percent in the US.[1]

Table 5.1
Residential property price gains 1995–2003

% Property prices	Cumulative	1995–2003 p.a.	2002 p.a.	2003 p.a.
US	61	6.1	6.9	8.0
Japan	-24	-3.3	-4.6	-5.8
Germany	-2	-0.2	1.0	-1.0
UK	146	11.9	23.9	10.0
France	60	6.1	6.7	16.4
Italy	42	4.5	10.0	10.7
Canada	42	4.5	10.3	11.0
Spain	122	10.5	17.4	17.3
Netherlands	110	10.2	4.5	3.6
Australia	110	10.2	18.5	18.9
Switzerland	3	0.4	4.9	2.8
Belgium	52	5.5	6.5	7.6
Sweden	8	7.8	9.2	6.1
Ireland	193	14.4	14.2	13.9
New Zealand	59	6.0	10.0	20.0

Source: Bank for International Settlements 2004 Annual Report (p. 138) and *OECD Economic Outlook* (75), June 2004.

Another study based on rents found house prices–rents to be 20 percent above equilibrium in Britain and Spain and 7 percent in the US.[2] This study was based on 2002 values so, with rents relatively static and prices up smartly since then, overvaluations will have grown significantly. Owner-occupiers have been actively trading up in many countries and second homes have become more popular. Investors have also been avid buyers as property has taken over from stocks as the "hot" investment. Many are "pension refugees" who have abandoned payments into pensions. In Australia one household in six reportedly now owns an investment property.[3]

So what is driving price rises? On the demand side it is mainly low interest rates, low unemployment, rising incomes, increased migration, and expectations of future price appreciation. And on the supply side, new building is constrained by planning and zoning restrictions as well as the time it takes to build.

The flaw in the picture though is those five words above, *expectations of future price appreciation.* In any asset market, whenever price appreciation becomes the main reason for people buying, the market is in danger of becoming a bubble. We must suspect a bubble if homeowners are regarding housing primarily as an investment, rather than as a place to live, and if investors are paying little attention to rental yields and are focused mostly on capital gains.

A detailed survey of US homebuyers in 2002 found some shocking evidence of high future price expectations (see Table 5.2), which make

Table 5.2
Housing expectations survey 2002

	Orange County	San Francisco	Boston	Milwaukee
Average annual appreciation 1982 Q1–2003 Q1	5.6%	7.1%	8.25%	5.6%
Expectations for appreciation				
– over next 12 months	10.5%	5.8%	7.2%	8.9%
– average over next 10 years	13.1%	15.7%	14.6%	11.7%
% of respondents expecting a rise over "the next several years"	89.7%	90.5%	83.1%	95.2%

Source: Karl E. Case, John M. Quigley, and Robert J. Shiller, "Home-Buyers, Housing and the Macroeconomy," in Anthony Richards and Tim Robinson (eds), *Asset Prices and Monetary Policy*, Reserve Bank of Australia, 2004, pp 149–88.

little sense based on long-term data. The authors asked 500 recent homebuyers in four areas—Orange County, San Francisco, Boston, and Milwaukee—about their expectations for prices in the next 12 months and over the next 10 years. Over the previous 21 years actual price appreciation ranged between 5.6 percent and 8.2 percent per annum in these four regions, yet house price expectations for the next 10 years ranged from 11.7 percent to 15.7 percent per annum. In Boston nearly 17 percent doubted whether prices would rise over the next several years, but that left 83 percent who thought they would. And in the other areas, 90 percent or more of respondents expected price gains.

Such surveys are worrying, not only because expectations are so much higher than past performance, despite the fact that overall inflation is lower, but also because people do not seem to recognize that the valuations of houses are already high. It appears that we have difficulty appreciating that housing markets, like most markets, exhibit cycles, so that a period of strongly rising prices leading to high valuations is likely, more often than not, to be followed by a period of slowly rising prices or even falls. In all four areas surveyed prices have risen strongly for at least the last seven years. But three of the four saw significant declines in the early 1990s. Prices in Los Angeles fell the most, 29 percent in nominal terms and 40 percent in real terms between 1988 and 1996. The exception was Milwaukee, which tends to have slow but steady price appreciation in line with incomes. Despite the evidence of cycles, Americans appear to believe that the market, nationwide, has become like Milwaukee at double speed.

THE DANGER FROM HOUSING BUBBLES

Bubbles in housing markets played a major role in the economic cycle at the end of both the 1970s and the 1980s. One study covering 15 countries found 29 "busts" in the last 30 years, defined as declines in real house prices greater than 13 percent (see Table 5.3). The average decline was 27 percent spread over 4½ years. Of course nominal prices fell by less, if at all, because of the effects of inflation. At the moment optimists on housing tend to discount these episodes because, with

Table 5.3

House price busts

Country	Date	Depth* (%)	Duration (Qtrs)
Australia	1974–78	16.1	19
	1981–86	35.1	20
Belgium	1979–84	32.7	20
Canada	1981–83	15.5	9
	1989–91	15.2	10
Denmark	1973–74	13.7	4
	1979–82	35.5	15
	1976–90	31.1	19
Finland	1974–79	27.0	20
	1989–93	50.5	16
Germany	1973–77	26.2	16
	1992–	28.2	40
Ireland	1979–86	26.2	27
Italy	1980–86	35.8	22
	1992–98	28.0	24
Japan	1973–77	28.2	16
	1991–	27.3	44
Netherlands	1978–82	50.1	19
Norway	1976–83	15.8	11
	1986–93	48.2	26
Spain	1978–82	32.0	16
	1991–97	21.2	21
Sweden	1979–85	40.4	25
	1990–93	30.1	14
Switzerland	1973–76	26.8	10
	1989–93	27.4	16
	1994–97	15.8	11
UK	1973–77	33.6	15
	1989–93	29.6	17
Average		**27.2**	**18**

* Peak to trough decline in real house prices.

Source: Goldman Sachs, *Global Economics Weekly*, April 30th, 2003 (p 7).

only a few exceptions, they occurred under the duress of a combination of high interest rates and a weak economy. And with inflation low, there is a widespread view that this particular combination looks unlikely in the near future.

However, it is not clear whether buyers in recent years have fully appreciated that interest rates were being held at unusually low levels. As rates normalize and especially if they need to go significantly above neutral at some point, people may be caught out. There are also examples of countries suffering house price busts due to weak economic growth, even with low or even very low interest rates, such as in Japan and Germany. The problem is that if house price expectations turn negative for any reason, cutting interest rates will not necessarily help the market.

Rising house prices are feeding back into consumer spending through the wealth effects described earlier, pulling down household savings rates. Mortgage equity withdrawal (MEW for short) has soared in the last three years, in 2003 reaching over 4 percent of household disposable income in the US and more than 6 percent in the UK. As recently as 1999 households were only withdrawing about 1 percent in both countries, while in the mid-1990s MEW was actually negative, meaning that households were putting money into housing on a net basis (in other words, saving for deposits). MEW of 4–6 percent of household spending does not necessarily mean that all of the money is going into spending on goods and services. Estimates suggest that only about 10–20 percent is directly spent. People may also be buying shares or other assets, or simply holding more bank deposits. Some people use mortgage equity withdrawal to pay down other debts, often those at higher interest rates, thereby reducing their cost of borrowing. But there is little doubt that consumer spending would have been much more subdued in recent years without the housing boom.

What happens if house prices stop rising? Initially, mortgage equity withdrawal may stay relatively strong. People are still catching up to the reality of the increased value of their house and so remortgage activity may stay high, as more and more people take advantage of the increased asset value. But if MEW stays constant at 4–6 percent of incomes, there is no *new* spending from that source so consumer spending growth and

GDP growth will start to slow down. A fall in MEW, very likely if house prices decline, would make that slowdown worse. Still, the effect on consumer spending through reduced MEW is likely to be gradual and could easily be offset by easier monetary policy, provided that the central banks spot what is happening in sufficient time.

However, an outright fall in house prices of any size could have a strong impact on the economy, working through a second channel, consumer wealth and confidence. Low savings rates reflect people's confidence that their wealth level looks good and is reasonably secure. But a fall in house prices would be a serious threat to many people's wealth, especially since housing wealth is geared; that is, most homeowners have a mortgage. People who bought years ago and have substantial accumulated equity, or those with only small mortgages, may be unfazed. Those who bought recently, especially if they have a large mortgage, could quickly be under water.

There is a third linkage between strong house prices and the economy, through construction spending. US house building has been strong throughout the economic slowdown in recent years, helping to moderate the recession. Similarly, in Spain and Australia house building is a major prop for the economy. In the UK planning restrictions mean that there has been little impact in terms of building new houses, though money spent on extending and improving houses has gone up. If house prices fall, house building will likely decline too, which could have important ramifications.

CAN HIGHER HOUSE PRICES BE JUSTIFIED?

During a bubble period, people always have plenty of reasons for why prices should be higher than in the past. Structural changes in demand do occur, of course, and can explain prices in particular regions. The explosion of jobs and wealth in Silicon Valley naturally boosted San Francisco property prices, for example. And increased immigration is probably important for London and Sydney. But the most important reason advanced at the moment to justify a higher level of house prices is low interest rates.[4] According to this view the lower cost of mortgages in a low interest rate world means that the demand for housing is likely to be permanently stronger, implying higher levels of the house price–earnings ratio and lower rental yields.

In its crude form this argument can be quickly rejected. If people are buying houses when interest rates are low while still expecting past rates of capital appreciation, they are clearly deluded. A world of 2 percent per annum inflation is likely to see the value of the average house doubling only every 20–30 years, far slower than in the last few decades. Moreover, interest rates have been unusually low in relation to inflation in recent years. Either they will rise, making housing less attractive, or inflation will drop still further, also limiting the upside for housing. If prices are overvalued now and need to correct downward, there could be no gain at all, even over a much longer period.

However, there are two other, more sophisticated arguments for why lower interest rates boost house price valuations, one of which is probably correct and the other probably not. The likely correct one is that, when interest rates were high in the past, people could not afford large mortgages because of the size of the monthly payment. Lower interest rates mean that monthly payments are lower now as the *real* cost of a mortgage is spread more evenly over its term. So people can afford to borrow more.

But note that the overall cost of the mortgage does not change. Instead of the mortgage payment diminishing rapidly as a proportion of earnings, it remains onerous for much longer. So lower interest rates do not make housing a better investment than before, just easier to invest in. Still, this could justify a somewhat higher level of house prices (in relation to earnings or rents) than before, particularly in the UK. However, in countries that provide tax relief against interest payments, for example the US and the Netherlands, there is an offset, since lower nominal interest rates reduce the tax benefit.

The argument that I believe is incorrect is the claim that, because we are living in a world of lower *real* interest rates, this in itself means that house valuations should be higher. At first hearing, this sounds right. For the owner-occupiers, the cost of buying housing services (to use the economists' jargon) is lower. And the investor in housing can secure a flow of rental payments with a cheaper mortgage. However, there is a particular reason why real interest rates are lower: The risk of a new bout of high inflation is now seen as small. But a lower inflation risk premium is *bad* news for housing as an investment. In comparing housing with other investments, one of its best attributes is that it provides inflation protection. If inflation is going to be low, or there is a threat of deflation, housing is much less attractive as an asset.

For Ireland and Spain, entry into EMU has been an important factor in their housing bubbles, by bringing interest rates down below what would otherwise be likely. Both countries have been growing much more strongly than the average for Europe and with higher inflation. But with interest rates set for the whole region, (one-size-fits-all) real interest rates have been low. In Spain absolute house prices are still below neighboring France (and of course are much lower than in the UK), but Irish prices are now relatively high compared with Europe as a whole. Spain has been enjoying a building boom, but building in Ireland has been unable to keep up with the inflow of population.

As long as economic growth continues and interest rates stay low, it may be possible for house prices to remain relatively high and indeed rise further. But on top of the good fundamentals are clear signs of a bubble mentality. A study by the Bank for International Settlements (BIS) found that historically the main influences on house prices were income gains, real interest rates, and stock prices. Using this model to assess the current situation, the study concluded that in four out of six countries examined, the US, UK, the Netherlands, and Australia, prices appear to have increased by more than warranted by the set of fundamental determinants considered. Of the other two, Ireland's gains were justified by its stellar economic growth performance, while Canada's house price growth was inexplicably lagging behind what the model predicted. But the data for this study only went up to 2001. In all these countries, house prices have risen much faster than earnings since then, suggesting that current price levels may be still further out of line, except for Canada, which is enjoying some healthy price increases and may soon conform to the model's expectations.[5]

In Australia house prices reached over 8 times earnings by the end of 2003, compared with 6.5 times at the last peak in 1989. But in early

2004, following hikes in official interest rates to 5.25 percent at the end of 2003, there have been tentative signs that the boom is going into reverse. Although official data for the whole country show a 2.5 percent rise in Q1 2004 (and 18 percent year on year), some industry sources suggest that prices in Sydney and Melbourne fell 8 percent and 13 percent respectively in Q1, with the decline led by falls in the prices of new condominiums as buy-to-let investment slowed.[6] It is too early to be sure whether this is really the beginning of a new trend, though the Governor of the Reserve Bank of Australia, Ian Macfarlane, who began to warn of the risks of a decline in prices in early 2003, has seized on it and argued that prices could fall further. Meanwhile, interest rate policy is hostage to house price trends more than ever. If house prices began a generalized decline, interest rates are unlikely to climb higher and could even be cut in 2005. But if the housing market stays strong, further rate rises are likely.

Australia is at the forefront of the world house price bubble at present and the behavior of Sydney and Melbourne house prices is being closely watched in other countries. It may prove that the combination of mild rate rises and strong warnings from the Reserve Bank will achieved the desired soft landing. A continuing buoyant economy could enable prices to correct modestly and allow time for earnings to catch up. However, house prices start from high levels and the market is very vulnerable to a sharp correction. Moreover, high rates of construction mean that new supply will continue to come on stream for some time and rents for condominiums are falling. Indeed, in Melbourne a new 88-story apartment tower is under construction. Unfortunately, the construction of large prestige buildings often marks the end of a boom: the Empire State Building in New York, for example, was begun in 1929 and the Canary Wharf Tower in London in the late 1980s.

In all the countries affected by bubbles, the risk of a major reversal in the market's direction is all the greater, the more inflated house prices, and price expectations, become. If house purchases are based mainly on expectations of house price gains and speculative behavior becomes widespread, the market is particularly vulnerable. If house prices did suddenly lurch downward, there is a real danger that expectations could change completely and that optimism could be replaced by pessimism and fear. At that point, even sharp cuts in interest rates might not be enough to stop prices falling substantially. Unfortunately, at the time of writing house price bubbles are still inflating in most countries and nowhere more so than in the UK.

6 BRITAIN NEARS THE TOP

The average British house, now worth about £140,000, would have sold for under £4,000 in 1965, an increase of 37 times, according to the Nationwide index. Over the same period the consumer price index increased about 12 times, so that in real terms house prices have roughly tripled. This equates to a return of about 2.9 percent per annum above inflation, though of course owners have also had the benefit of living in the house or receiving rent over the same period (less maintenance costs). However, most of the rise in real terms has occurred in just the last eight years. As recently as 1995 house prices were up only 40 percent in real terms compared with 1965, an annual rise of a fraction over 1 percent.

Real house prices have not marched steadily up every year but instead followed a pronounced cyclical pattern, broadly corresponding to the UK business cycle. In fact, analyzed in real terms, the UK has suffered four bubbles and three busts in the last 40 years (see Table 6.1). Three long upswings, prior to 1973, from 1982–9, and from 1995–2004, saw prices approximately double on each occasion. The two earlier long upswings were followed by major bear markets, with declines of 32 percent and 37.1 percent in real terms. The late 1970s saw a shorter upswing and correspondingly smaller bear market.

Actual prices did not fall in the recessions of 1975 and 1980 because underlying annual inflation was relatively high, 24 percent in 1974 and 18 percent in 1980. In 1990, however, inflation was only about 9 percent per annum and quickly fell to under 4 percent per annum by 1992. The result was that the correction to nominal house prices, in the aftermath of the severe 1990s recession, was a painful 20 percent from the peak in Q3 1989 to the low in Q1 1993.

The UK is particularly prone to housing cycles for two reasons. One is that most houses are financed on floating interest rates. So when the

Table 6.1
House price cycles in real terms

Period	No. of quarters	Change
1957 Q3–1973 Q3	64	+125.0%
1973 Q3–1977 Q2	15	-32.0%
1977 Q2–1979 Q4	10	+32.7%
1979 Q4–1982 Q2	10	-17.8%
1982 Q2–1989 Q2	28	+80.0%
1989 Q2–1995 Q3	25	-37.1%
1995 Q3–2004 Q2	36+	+122.0%

Bank of England lowers or raises interest rates to control the economy, one of the major transmission mechanisms is through the effects on mortgage payments and on the housing market.

The other reason is that the supply of housing in Britain is exceptionally slow to respond to higher prices because of draconian planning controls. Glance out of an aircraft coming into land in Britain, even southern England, and there appears to be no shortage of farmland available. But there is huge resistance to more development, both from environmental pressure groups and NIMBY local resistance (Not In My Back Yard). Long ago, local authorities designated "green belt" areas that have become virtually sacrosanct. More recent restrictions such as "village envelopes" have prevented the growth of villages and can only be overcome at great effort and cost. As a result, high and rapidly rising house prices have had no impact at all on supply.[1]

BUBBLE CHECK

Referring back to our checklist of bubble characteristics in Chapter 1, the current UK house price boom fits very closely. Valuations are now historically high, for example in relation to earnings (see Chart 6.1). During house price booms the ratio has typically risen to over 4 times

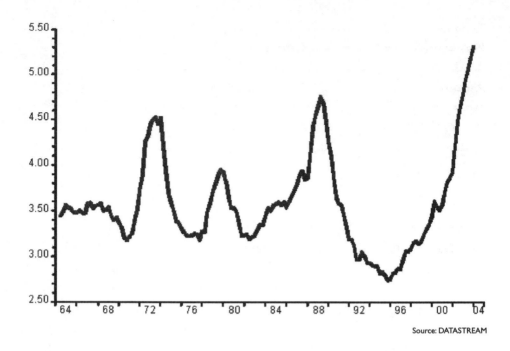

Source: DATASTREAM

Chart 6.1
UK: House prices/average earnings

earnings and then, during the downswing, it usually falls back to the
3–3.5 times range. In the mid-1990s the ratio fell to an unusually low
level, only 2.8 times, reflecting a widespread reluctance to buy houses
after the substantial decline in prices in the early 1990s. At that time,
expectations for future house price increases were very low. Many potential first-time buyers were reluctant to move into the market and existing owners were unwilling to trade up. Many people still rued the day
when they had bought during the last bubble in the late 1980s and
investment buyers were comparatively rare.

When prices first began to pick up in 1994, the increases were
merely taking valuations back to average levels. But since about 1998
the ratio has moved into "expensive" territory and in 2003–4 it moved
to levels higher than ever seen before. The house price boom began in
London and the South East, but has increasingly rippled out through
the country and in 2002–4 most of the big gains were outside the
South East.

Prices are also high relative to rents. Yields (gross annual rent divided by the value of the property) on prime London flats have declined from a relatively high 8–10 percent in the mid-1990s to only 3.5–5 percent currently. The Investment Property Databank calculates average yields for the whole country at 6.1 percent at end 2003, down from 7.3 percent in 2001.[2]

The economy has been healthy for a prolonged period, with the current upswing now more than 12 years old. The UK economy saw only modest weakness in 2001–3, with a check in the downward trend in unemployment but no increase. Consumer confidence has held up relatively well.

The new element in this bubble is the increase in immigration to Britain, particularly the South East, associated with asylum seekers and the new EU nations as well as the attractions of the London job markets. But house prices have risen almost everywhere now, even in areas where migration is not significant. The paradigm shift in this case is perhaps the view that "housing is the best pension" after the disappointment with stock markets and the worries over company pension schemes. More people have been drawn into the market, especially investors but also owner-occupiers, increasingly buying for capital gain rather than simply for living space. Entrepreneurs offering instant buy-to-let portfolios have become increasingly common and seminars on how to build a property empire have proliferated.

Media interest has been intense, with endless property sections in newspapers and a plethora of new TV programs with titles such as *Property Ladder* and *Location, Location, Location.* There have been plenty of warnings of a bubble, but there has also been a considerable media focus on the gains being made and the riches available to people who have geared up and bought a portfolio of houses. On the lending side there is overwhelming evidence of rapid mortgage growth, with unprecedented debt-to-income ratios and high loan-to-value ratios. There are also new lending policies on buy-to-let mortgages, now available on much more advantageous terms than a few years ago, as well as aggressive competition between lenders. Household debt has soared to new highs.

Meanwhile, monetary policy has stayed fairly relaxed. The Bank of England has not attempted to rein in the bubble, because of its focus on consumer price inflation, which remains low. While this is not necessarily the wrong policy (we will return to this issue), it has certainly not prevented massive new mortgage lending. The regulatory authorities have had only a limited and rather recent effect in tightening credit criteria for lending. Some banks have tightened their policies, but very attractive introductory mortgage deals are still available, including large interest rate discounts and over 100 percent financing. As we discussed earlier, the UK household savings rate has fallen to only 5 percent, the same level as during the last housing bubble. Finally, the pound has been strong on a trade-weighted basis for a number of years and the current account deficit is expanding.

IS THIS TIME DIFFERENT?

Three times before UK house price upswings have been followed by a major correction. Those who believe that risks are low this time, or expect only a small correction of perhaps 10–15 percent, base their optimism on one or more of the following arguments. Many cite evidence to show that underlying demand for housing is increasing, particularly in the South of England. Others focus on the argument that there is no likely trigger for a house price correction. Finally, some rely on the assertion that lower interest rates justify permanently higher house prices, relative to earnings or rents. That claim we discussed in the last chapter and found that it is questionable for any country. What about the other two arguments in the British case?

Many of the claims about demographics and underlying demand are grounded in reality. There has been a growing tendency for people to want to live in London and the South East of England. London has become an increasingly cosmopolitan city, led by the financial sector and global business services as well as knowledge- and media-based activities. In the late 1990s young people flocked to London from all over Europe and elsewhere, drawn by an exciting lifestyle, plentiful jobs, and the English language, second language for so many people. For a while after the stock market collapsed the jobs dwindled and some people left, driving down rents on luxury apartments and leaving many restaurants emptier. But with the world economy recovering, London's allure is returning.

There are also demographic changes such as an increase in the number of divorces and a growing desire for young people to live in their own flats rather than at home or in house shares. Increasingly, parents buy properties for their children to use when they are at university or just starting work. Some have even been buying when their children are only 15 or so, though this is surely a clear case of bubble mentality. There is also a strong trend for many people to seek larger houses to bring up families, or as second homes. This latter works both ways, with some people living in the country choosing to buy flats in London or other large cities to escape daily commuting while others owning property in and around London have been buying holiday homes, lured by the prospect of weekends in the country and the possibility of holiday lets to pay the bills.

However, there are serious problems with all of these arguments as a justification for hugely higher house prices. For a start, most people were not nearly so keen on buying when prices were at half current levels, as recently as 1996–8. Now, with prices high, they believe that they must buy now or pay even more later. It is very difficult to deny that a crucial factor in this is expectations of future price appreciation. Living in the country and owning a pied-à-terre in London seems like a perfect strategy if the price of both is going to appreciate for ever. What is there to lose? The holiday home not only earns a tidy sum on a few lets in July and August, but also will be up in value over a few years. The happy owners can enjoy both properties and also smile in the knowledge that, even if their pension scheme is looking decidedly shaky, having two properties will set them up for retirement.

Most people do realize, of course, that double-digit gains are impossible every year and that the last few years have been exceptional. But many, nevertheless, still believe that even if prices fall a little in the short term, they will be higher in 10 years' time. And yet this is far from guaranteed. It was the same belief that made people confident about stocks in 1999–2000.

Before turning to why prices could fall, we should note two important offsets to the structural increases in underlying demand discussed above. One is that the tax treatment of property in the UK is no longer as favorable as in the past. In the 1970s, the mortgage interest on any size of mortgage could be set against tax. In the 1980s, this benefit began to be restricted, though it was still an important tax break during the house price boom of the 1980s. It was finally phased out completely in the tax year 2000–1. The Bank of England has calculated that the change in tax treatment between 1990 and 2000 effectively raised the borrowing cost by about 3 percent per annum and that this should have *reduced* the equilibrium real house price by 9 percent.[3]

Meanwhile, stamp duty on the purchase of houses has been increased sharply, which again should have lowered the value of housing. Stamp duty used to be charged at 1 percent, but only on properties valued above £60,000, still a high value in the 1980s. Now, with the average property up to about £140,000, only a small minority of transactions are excluded. Moreover, buyers paying £250,000 or more pay a 3 percent rate, rising to 4 percent over £500,000. Overall then, the effective rate is probably at least 1 percent higher than 15 years ago, which is calculated to have the effect of lowering house prices by 3 percent.[4]

Finally, the local authority council tax on property values should also have reduced house prices, by raising the cost of trading up to a more valuable house. In the late 1980s Britain had no tax on housing values because the poll tax (a flat-rate tax on residents) had just replaced the old rates system. With council tax running at something like ¼–½ percent of housing values, this should be enough to pull prices back by some 2–5 percent compared with the 1980s.

Overall then, these tax changes ought to be reducing house price levels by about 15 percent relative to incomes or rents. Housing does still have tax advantages, since owner-occupied homes are free of capital gains tax, while foreign investors do not pay capital gains tax on investment property. But these arrangements have not changed recently so, in principle, cannot justify a rise in prices.

One thing that has changed over the last 15 years is the introduction of a favorable regulatory and tax regime for investors, following an overhaul of tenancy arrangements in the late 1980s (too late to have much impact on the bubble then). Landlords now enjoy straightforward treatment of tax on rental property and can turf out nonpaying tenants relatively easily. However, the surge in ownership of investment property is as much a cause for worry as a good explanation for why high prices are justified. Rents have been showing much less buoyancy than prices and there are signs that inexperienced investors are being carried away by recent strong capital gains returns.

The second major offset to the arguments about the excess demand for housing is the number of extensions that people have made to their houses. This point is often overlooked, but extensions effectively increase the housing stock, even if there are few new houses being built. And the high value of housing (as well as high stamp duty) makes extending especially attractive. My guess is that the majority of properties in the South of England, where prices are particularly high relative to building work, have been extended in the last 20 years and many in recent years. If every three-bedroom house is extended to provide a fourth bedroom and another downstairs living room, in effect there is 25 percent more housing available. Of course, not every house has been or indeed could be extended, and the process has been going on over a very long period, but I would estimate that the increase in the housing stock from extensions is as large an effect as that from new building.

Ultimately though, to see how much the current bubble rests on high price expectations rather than fundamentals, consider the following questions. If people believed that housing was not a good investment, how much housing would they buy then? Would they increase their debt to secure a larger house, a better area, or a second home, knowing that the mortgage interest payments were just another cost, like electricity bills, and not a promising investment? Or would they limit their aspirations? When the price of something more than doubles and people want more instead of less, we should strongly suspect that the market is in a bubble.

WHERE IS THE TRIGGER?

It is certainly true that a trigger for a major correction is less obvious than in prior episodes. Past house price busts have been associated with both rising interest rates and a recession. In the early 1990s, when the

UK last experienced a house price bust, not only was the economy weak but interest rates were held higher than they otherwise would have been by Britain's membership of the Exchange Rate Mechanism. Currently, if the economy slows, the Bank of England is likely to cut interest rates quickly.

This, incidentally, is one of the greatest risks of Britain joining EMU. If Britain suffered a house price bust as a member of EMU, interest rates might need to go close to zero to deal with the aftermath and, unless the rest of Europe was weak at precisely the same time, rates would not be cut that low. In a worst-case scenario Britain could face a Japan-style depression, including a ruptured financial sector and a severe economic downturn. Still, at the time of writing it looks highly unlikely that Britain will join EMU any time soon, so we need not fear that this will be the trigger.

Some people go so far as to argue that the economy is very unlikely to go into recession. It is true that inflation is not currently a problem so, in contrast to past episodes, there is no immediate likelihood that the Bank of England will want to raise rates sharply above neutral levels to slow the economy. However, it is surely brave to believe that, after more than 12 years of economic upswing, growth can go on for ever and inflation will never return. It may not be obvious where the downswing will come from or why the central bank should raise rates sharply and it may still be a couple of years away or more, but it would be truly remarkable if a recession continued to be avoided for many more years.

Moreover, with house price valuations now so extreme, one very real possibility is that the market starts to fall on its own, and this in itself could be the trigger for a weakening economy. But why would house prices start falling on their own, without a trigger or event? The answer is a combination of price expectations and underlying demand. People may start to see existing prices as simply too high to allow for much further growth. There are already signs of this in the higher-priced parts of southern England, where prices overall have been relatively stable over the last two years and some areas have seen price falls. This end of the market is very much influenced by City bonuses, which went through a rough patch in 2001–3, though they picked up in 2004. At the bottom end of the market the number of first-time buyers has dropped off sharply and the average age has risen, reflecting difficulties in raising the necessary deposit or borrowing sufficient money.

Another possibility is that the trigger for a collapse of UK house prices comes from so-called contagion. When most of the countries in East Asia suffered a crisis in 1997–8, the trigger was a crisis in Thailand. And because some of the characteristics of the Thai crisis were replicated elsewhere, the crisis quickly spread. Some observers believe that a collapse of house prices in Australia could spook the British market, though there is much less new building in Britain.

Everybody's favorite scenario is that prices flatten out or fall marginally, allowing a "soft landing." However, markets do not often behave like this, especially if many people have bought primarily for capital gain. Moreover, because wages are growing only relatively slowly at present, in contrast to past episodes, it would take many years for the house price–earnings ratio to fall or rental yields to rise (through higher rents alone). If the market is 30 percent overvalued it would take nearly seven years to correct through earnings growth alone. Rental yields point the same way. A yield of 6 percent per annum does not sound much different from a yield of 8 percent. But there is a huge difference if the actual money rent does not change and the yield changes through the price adjusting. For yields to move from 6 percent to 8 percent (still under historical averages), prices would have to fall by 25 percent.

THE DOWNSIDE RISKS ARE CONSIDERABLE

Low inflation means that a correction in house prices now would be potentially much more severe and long-lasting even than in the early 1990s. Suppose that prices fall 30 percent over the four years to 2008. This would almost certainly be associated with a weak economy, so average earnings growth would naturally slow from its current 3–4 percent per annum rate, perhaps to 2 percent. That 30 percent fall, combined with the earnings growth over the period, would take house prices back to close to the average house price–earnings ratio. So it would be reasonable to expect some resumption of price growth from there. If, starting in 2009, house prices rose at the rate of earnings growth, 2 percent per annum, they would take a further 15 years to return to today's level. A house worth £300,000 now would be worth just £283,000 in 2024 and would not exceed today's level until 2027. Note that this is by no means the worst-case scenario, since housing valuations could very easily fall below average levels, as they did in the early 1990s, while earnings growth might slow still further.

If prices are the same or slightly lower in 20 years' time, this might not worry some owner-occupiers. Most people will have bought before the peak of the bubble so that, while they will see some erosion of their equity and perhaps suffer some disappointment, they may not be losing much. The element of disappointment could be important, of course, if they were in some way relying on future appreciation to help fund their retirement. It is also true, however, that in this scenario mortgage rates are likely to be lower even than in 2003, reducing mortgage service costs. But the cost of maintaining a house is often overlooked in making these comparisons and, in reality, may amount to 1–2 percent of the value annually over time. Think of the need to repair roofs and windows, redecorate inside and out, as well as periodically replace kitchens, bathrooms, central heating systems, and appliances.

For property investors the 30 percent decline scenario above would, to say the least, be a huge disappointment, because there would be no capital gain for more than 20 years. Of course, provided that they could find tenants and provided that rents did not fall, their net rental yield should be positive so there would be some income after costs, though not much given the low level of yields. It is difficult to define exactly where investors would end up, because a great deal depends on how big a loan they have and what rent they could obtain. But there is no doubt that this is what disappointed investors call "a very long-term investment," or in other words a mistake. The choice is either sell and accept the loss or wait it out, but then miss the opportunity to make money elsewhere.

In 2004 all the main UK house price indices are still showing substantial gains. Real and nominal interest rates have begun to rise, but remain relatively low in historical terms. And with the world economic upswing and recovery in the financial sector, optimism has picked up, unemployment is falling, and City bonuses are on the rise. But later in 2004, or perhaps in 2005, my guess is that the bubble will run out of momentum. One popular view is that prices will simply plateau out, without a major decline. However, after a bubble, significant declines are more likely with or without a trigger.

A collapse in house prices would weaken the economy through slower consumer spending growth and would threaten a recession. The way out would be for interest rates to be cut, possibly close to zero as in Japan in recent years, and also for the pound to fall sharply, as in 1992–3. But it could be a very difficult few years and would likely see inflation stay low (despite the devaluation) or even present a threat of deflation.

COULD THE BRITISH BUBBLE HAVE BEEN AVOIDED?

Preventing the bubble inflating would have required action starting as long ago as 1998–2000. House prices moved up to bubble levels in London first, rippled out to the South East in the following couple of years, and then spread to the whole country in 2002–3. A higher path of interest rates would have limited the bubble, but there is a danger that economic growth would have been lower and therefore unemployment higher. And since consumer price inflation is still not a problem in 2003–4, even with this fairly robust growth, it is certainly arguable that sacrificing growth to keep house prices under control would not have been a good tradeoff. Moreover, pushing interest rates to high levels to slow the house price boom might have taken the pound higher still against the euro, hurting manufacturing even worse than it already had been. It is easy to see, therefore, why the Bank of England was unwilling to confront the housing bubble directly. However, if my worst fears come true and Britain does face a house price slump and a recession at some point in the next few years, we may well look back and say that the tradeoff would have been worthwhile.

Nevertheless, I think a more fruitful approach is to ask whether measures other than higher interest rates could have been taken to slow house price increases. Much more strident warnings from people in authority might have helped. Members of the Bank of England's Monetary Policy Committee have sounded warnings from time to time, but the overall effect was muted for a long time. This changed in June 2004 when the Governor of the Bank of England, Mervyn King, made a series of widely reported speeches warning that prices are high and could fall. However, the danger is that these warnings have come too late. Government ministers have been almost entirely silent, doubtless not wishing to spoil the party and keeping their fingers crossed that a house price slump will not get in the way of reelection. They did raise stamp duty and they have presided over a sharp rise in council tax, but these measures have been swamped. Gordon Brown, the Chancellor, also commissioned studies on housing supply, the Barker report and the Miles report on the mortgage market.[5] But when Mervyn King belatedly began his public warnings, government ministers and officials played down the risks.

Stronger action could and probably should have been taken on the bank lending side. The bank supervisory authorities have warned about overlending on several occasions, but with limited effect. Banks feel comfortable with the risk they are taking, believing that even if house prices fall substantially and many people are faced with negative equity, defaults will be small, as is usually the case with mortgages.

One uncertainty here is the new bankruptcy rules, introduced in April 2004, making it less onerous for individuals to file for bankruptcy. The number of bankruptcies in Britain is already at high levels, despite a strong economy, low unemployment, and low interest rates, due to difficulties with nonmortgage debt. In a recession and a falling house price environment, the numbers would undoubtedly go much higher.

The fundamental problem, however, is that during a bubble, a bank supervisory approach that focuses only on the risks being faced by each institution may not take sufficient account of the overall volume of new lending. I hesitate to advocate new rules and regulations, though if the British market crashes in the next few years I suspect we will see some changes. They will be too late for this bubble.

7 A US BUBBLE?

While the bursting of Britain's bubble seems inevitable before long, a much greater danger, for America as well as for the whole world economy, is that the US is also developing a bubble. A US housing bust could easily trigger a recession and, as usual, it would be doubtful if the rest of the world could avoid recession too. Concerns about the US market began to surface as early as 2000–1 but, with price rises accelerating since then, the issue has moved to center stage.

Home prices rose 41.8 percent on average in the US over the last five years, well ahead of consumer price inflation of 12.6 percent. And in 2003, despite the dampener of the Iraq war, the increase was 8 percent. Some regions have seen much faster gains, with Massachusetts and California up around 75 percent and New Jersey and New York up over 60 percent (see Table 7.1). The average price of a Manhattan apartment touched almost $1 million in spring 2004, up 28 percent on a year earlier.

One of the difficulties in assessing the American housing market is that, to a much greater extent than in Britain, the US is a series of regional markets, with only limited correlation between them. Prices in Florida may respond to a boom in the North East, as people buy second homes or retirement homes. But a bubble in Manhattan has little resonance in Detroit. And in large parts of the country the supply response to rising prices is quite strong, reflecting the ample availability of land.

The nationwide index for US home prices has marched upward over the last 25 years, with prices never falling for more than a few months. Prices in certain areas, particularly on the coasts, have been much more volatile and have seen periodic bubbles and busts. Texas prices crashed after the fall in world oil prices in 1986, while California and New England fell sharply after the 1990 recession, with California affected strongly by the defense cutbacks following the fall of the Berlin Wall.

Table 7.1
House price appreciation: Top 10 states

%	5 years to December 2003
District of Columbia	90.0
Rhode Island	79.3
Massachusetts	77.1
California	75.7
New Hampshire	73.1
New Jersey	62.8
New York	61.5
Minnesota	58.0
Maine	56.7
Florida	53.2
US average	**41.8**
Consumer price inflation	12.6

However, just as in the UK prior to 1990, nationwide house prices have not fallen, because of the underpinning from ongoing consumer price inflation. Between Q1 1990 and Q1 1995 the nominal house price index climbed 7.6 percent. But with consumer price inflation of 17.9 percent, real house prices fell approximately 10 percent. In California the nominal price decline of about 10 percent over the same period translated to a 24 percent decline in real terms.

After the price correction of the early 1990s, the market picked up gradually in the mid-1990s and then took off from the late 1990s. The 61 percent increase over the last eight years is a smaller increase than in many other countries, but is well ahead of inflation of 20 percent. And most analyses now suggest that, on a nationwide basis, prices look high compared with past trends.[1]

The extent of the overvaluation is illustrated in Chart 7.1, showing the ratio of prices to rents and prices to the median income. Both ratios have been through cycles before, but are currently 10–15 percent *higher* than past cycle peaks and 20–25 percent above their averages. In prior

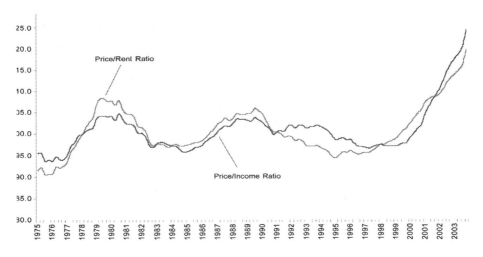

Source: GOLDMAN SACHS

Chart 7.1
US: House price ratios

housing market downturns in the 1980s and early 1990s, these ratios
fell about 10 percent over a period of three to five years to cyclical lows.
From current much higher levels, to return to past cyclical lows would
require a fall of 25–30 percent. In past episodes both incomes and rents
were rising with general inflation and cushioned the blow. But in
recent years median incomes and rents have been rising only very
slowly, so this would imply a nominal house price fall of perhaps 15–20
percent.

In some regions price rises have been much greater than the national
average and there is even stronger evidence of extreme valuations. For
example, the eight-year increase has been 107 percent in Massachusetts,
99 percent in California, and 75 percent in New Jersey and New York.
Meanwhile, an index of affordability produced by Fidelity National suggests that the typical consumer in Miami can afford only 83 percent of
the city's median house price. The figures in major West Coast cities are
even lower, for example 68 percent in Los Angeles and 63 percent in
San Francisco.[2]

California, New Jersey, New York, Massachusetts, and Florida are the
most worrisome states. They have had volatile house prices in the past
and, once again, seem to be relatively expensive. Though only a handful

of states, they comprise 30 percent of the total population, are important in influencing public opinion, and contain some of the most valuable real estate in the country.

However, some analysts question the idea of a housing bubble. For example, a report to Congress in 2003 argued that the case for a national bubble was unproven, though it did point to regional bubbles.[3] Skeptics tend to focus on the impact of low interest rates in justifying higher house prices, though, as I have argued above, this is a questionable justification for high valuations. But in any case, as house prices continue to climb, it becomes increasingly hard to argue that they are not overvalued.

OTHER SIGNS OF A BUBBLE

Are there other signs of a bubble? Referring to our checklist again, the picture is somewhat more mixed than in the UK. For example, the US is not several years into an economic upswing, as is common for a bubble. The current upswing only started in late 2001 and did not become strong until 2003. Nevertheless, the survey of expectations described in Chapter 5 suggests that confidence in house price inflation is well entrenched after 10 years of buoyant increases. And the 2001 recession was the mildest on record.

There has certainly been a major rise in lending, with mortgage debt up from $4,523 billion at the end of 1999 to $6,820 billion at the end of 2003. Of course, part of this increase reflects refinancing and mortgage equity withdrawal, but part will have fueled house price increases. While higher borrowing is linked to lower mortgage rates, it is also true that, as in Britain, mortgages are more easily obtainable than ever before.

An important change in the last decade or so is the increased importance of the secondary market for mortgages. Years ago mortgages were agreed by bank managers and then mostly held on the bank's books, so if the homeowner defaulted, the bank would face a loss. But now it is much more common for banks to originate mortgages and then sell them on to Fannie Mae or Freddie Mac.[4]

Congress created the Federal National Mortgage Corporation (Fannie Mae) in the 1930s to make loans to low-income Americans by agreeing to purchase mortgages from the originating banks. In 1970 another agency, the Federal Home Loan Mortgage Corporation (Freddie Mac), was set up to do much the same thing.

These institutions either hold the mortgages themselves, financed by issuing their own bonds, or turn them into "mortgage-backed securities" and sell them to investors. At the end of the 1980s they were buying up 30 percent of new mortgages, but further expansion was constrained by their ability to attract new investment capital.

Then in 1989, Congress instituted some technical changes that made Freddie and Fannie more attractive to investors, such as allowing them to customize securities at different levels of risk and return. Meanwhile, the regulators let pension funds and mutual funds class Fannie's debt as low risk. As a result of these changes, Freddie and Fannie have grown rapidly, buying up more and more mortgages. By 2004, their share of conventional mortgage debt had more than doubled to 70 percent.

Of course, to be eligible for purchase these mortgages have to meet strict "conforming" criteria. Moreover, the agencies themselves, which are privately owned, as well as investors in the mortgage-backed securities, would suffer if there was a serious rise in defaults. Nevertheless, it is hard to avoid the suspicion that loans are being made more easily now than in the past and this means more money chasing houses.

A 2003 survey of appraisers is revealing in this respect. Nearly three out of four randomly selected licenced appraisers told researchers that they had been pressured over the past year by a mortgage broker or loan officer to "hit a certain value." And if they ignored the pressure, they faced the risk of a loss of business. One common tactic is "pre-comping," where a loan officer asks in advance whether the appraiser thinks he or she can come up with comparable sales for a property to justify a specific target range for the mortgage. If the appraiser expresses doubts, the loan officer goes to another appraiser. Of the appraisers who reported pressure, 48 percent said that the overvaluations demanded were 1–10 percent above the true value of the property, while 43 percent said that they were 11–30 percent above market value.[5]

Returning to the checklist of bubble signs, in the US, just as in the UK, there has been much talk of structural changes in demand for housing, related to immigration and faster household growth. There has also been a shift to investment in housing as an alternative to stocks. And in some areas there have been signs of buyer frenzy. For example, the *Washington Post* reported that home buyers in Arlington, Virginia camped out overnight to be the first in the next morning's "open house."

The household savings rate is low. It was already down to 2 percent at the end of the stock market boom and, contrary to expectations, has stayed low. Meanwhile, consumer price inflation is subdued and monetary policy strongly stimulative. US mortgage rates averaged 7–8 percent for much of the 1990s but fell below 6 percent in 2002–4. Just as in Britain, there is a tendency to look at the monthly payment on a mortgage as the cost of buying a house, rather than making any allowance for the fact that, with interest rates lower because of lower inflation, the potential upside for housing values is correspondingly lower.

US homebuyers do of course enjoy tax relief on mortgage interest, though with lower interest rates and lower marginal tax rates this relief is worth less than in the past. However, one very important difference to Britain is that most mortgages in the US are at long-term fixed rates. And an unusual feature of the US mortgage market compared with other countries is that, while homeowners will never face a rise in their mortgage rate, they can take advantage of a cut, if interest rates fall enough to compensate for early repayment penalties. So as mortgage rates have come down in recent years, some homeowners have refinanced several times. We shall come back to this in relation to the rise in household debt and the implications for monetary policy, but one strong implication is that Americans have much less to fear from rising interest rates.

However, just as in Britain, if inflation fears resurface mortgage rates will go up sharply. In the US this is not so much because of a rise in official rates, but because long-term bond yields will reflect inflation fears. While existing homeowners will be unaffected, new buyers are likely to be deterred.

WHAT IF HOME PRICES FALL?

When the stock market bubble burst in 2000–2, the effect was to wipe about $5 trillion off US household wealth. It would take a 33 percent fall in home prices to have the same impact. A decline of this magnitude cannot be ruled out if valuation ratios returned to past cyclical lows, but it would only be likely in the context of a serious recession and a new rise in unemployment. However, as noted earlier, wealth effects from declining house prices are usually found to be more virulent than those from falling stock markets, so a fall of "only" 15–20 percent could present Mr. Greenspan, or his successors, with a similar headache to the aftermath of the stock crash.

But a housing crash would have other effects too. In the US, far more than in the UK, housing construction is a key driver of economic growth. In Britain, with a population of 60 million, around 180,000 new dwellings were constructed in 2003. The US, with under five times the population, built ten times more, around 1.8 million. And US house building has been booming in the last few years, reflecting strong demand and buoyant prices, helping to sustain economic growth.

In past housing downturns residential investment fell sharply, by 40 percent in 1980–82 and by 24 percent in 1988–91. This is reflected in the monthly housing starts data, which typically halve during recessions. However, starts only ticked down briefly in 2001 and have since risen close to past peaks (see Chart 7.2). Residential investment accounts for about 5 percent of GDP, so a severe house-building recession would be enough to cut GDP by 1–2 percent on its own.

Is there a danger of serious problems for banks if negative equity increases? In past housing recessions delinquency and foreclosure rates rose only modestly. For example, between 1988 and 1991, delinquency rates rose from 4.79 to 5.03 percent, while foreclosures increased from 0.27 to 0.34 percent.[6] This was in an environment of high unemployment and high mortgage rates, but still-rising nominal house prices.

A future housing bust in the US would likely be in the context of falling nominal house prices, rising unemployment, but low mortgage rates. Quite how this combination would play out is unclear. Homeowners still need somewhere to live and, if they could refinance their

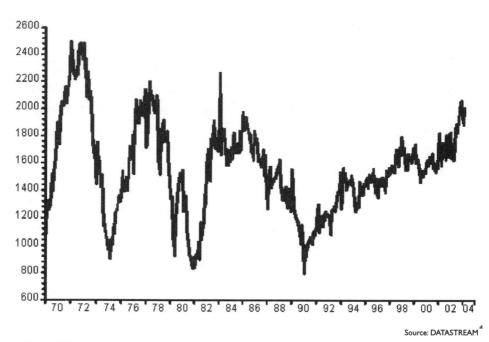

Source: DATASTREAM[A]

Chart 7.2
US: Housing starts

loan at a lower rate, they would probably struggle to get by, rather than defaulting. However, if nominal prices fall sufficiently and expectations for future house price growth turn negative, some people would walk away. And investors might be particularly likely to do so.

One strength of the US housing finance system is that the risk of mortgage defaults is spread around the capital markets rather than being mainly on banks' balance sheets. So banks are less at risk than in the past, while investors in mortgage-backed securities could face losses. Nevertheless, in practice banks hold substantial amounts of these securities, so they could still face problems in their investment portfolio.

At the end of 2003, mortgage securities issued by Freddie and Fannie totaled $5,600 billion, more than one and a half times the value of all US Treasury securities. In February 2003 OFHEO (the awkwardly named Office of Federal Housing Enterprise Oversight) published a report examining the implications of a default by Freddie Mac or Fannie Mae. The report made clear that the result would be a serious financial crisis and that the Federal Reserve would need to move quickly to limit the damage. Even though the report described this scenario as "remote," it sent shock waves through the markets and cost the OFHEO director his job, just 24 hours later.[7]

Although Freddie and Fannie are private companies, they are considered to be government sponsored and so their bonds trade at only modest spreads over US Treasuries. The risk of default is seen as very small, at least while house prices are rising, but also, in the event of trouble, there is a widespread view that the government would have to bail them out. The US government has periodically tried to make the point that the government does not guarantee this paper. But investors believe that politicians would not stand by and see the mortgage finance market collapse and people lose money on these bonds. If they did, the housing market would fall even further and the two-thirds of Americans who own houses would be deeply unhappy. Nevertheless, that does not mean that there might not be a crisis, or fears of a crisis, before the government stepped in.

Such a crisis would most likely take the form of a sharp rise in spreads on mortgage bonds, making mortgages more expensive. It is easy to imagine too that operational procedures would change in a housing bust. Just as we have seen companies report their profits more conservatively since the stock market bust, so the agencies and originating banks would tighten up their lending criteria. Banks would become less aggressive in their marketing and appraisers would be under pressure to be prudent rather than compliant. As a result, mortgages would become more difficult to obtain.

HOW LIKELY IS A BUST?

But how likely is a US housing bust? At the moment, valuations do not appear so high that there is an imminent danger of them turning down all on their own, taking the economy with them. Indeed, if the economy continues to grow and unemployment trends down, it seems to me more likely that home prices will continue to rise, inflating the bubble further. Good news on the economic front will support house prices, while rising mortgage rates (likely in a strong economic environment) will oppose them. The outcome will depend partly on how much mortgage rates do in fact rise, a question for the next chapter, but also whether the early signs of a bubble psychology, now evident in the US in some regions, extend further. If the bubble really gets going, rising interest rates may have little effect because people will be much more focused on quick gains.

The ideal outcome from here would be a period where home prices were broadly stable, allowing earnings and rents to catch up and valuations to moderate. A small fall in the market of 5–10 percent would help that process along without causing too much hardship, though a nationwide 5–10 percent fall would almost certainly imply falls of 10–20 percent in parts of California and New England.

The most dangerous scenario is if house valuations are still extended when the next shock hits the US economy. With consumer price inflation low, house prices will almost certainly fall in the next recession, potentially making the recession much worse. They would also be vulnerable if interest rates rose sharply, most likely if inflation revives unexpectedly quickly. But in this environment stock prices would likely be falling too, so that the economy would face a double dose of asset price effects, adding up to a much more lethal mixture than in the aftermath of the stock market bust.

In short, the bubble in housing is likely to become a worrying complication for the Fed in coming years and monetary policy will be seriously challenged. The continued health of the US economy is dependent on developments in home prices more than ever before. But rising home prices are not the only complication for monetary policy makers. A second, closely related headache is the rapid increase in household debt in recent years.

8 HOUSEHOLD DEBT AND MONETARY POLICY

I n the five years to 2003, US household debt rose by 52 percent and the ratio to income reached a record 132 percent. In the UK debt jumped 63 percent over the same period, while in Australia it rose even faster, by a whopping 90 percent. In relation to household incomes, debts have soared to over 150 percent in both countries. By way of contrast, Japan and Germany, where house prices are weak, have seen much smaller increases in debt and their ratios to incomes have remained stable (see Table 8.1).

Part of the rise in debt can be attributed to a greater proportion of the population owning their own homes. And part is due to individuals taking out mortgages on investment properties. However, the bulk of the increase in debt can only be explained in relation to higher home prices. New buyers and people trading up are forced to take on

Table 8.1

Household debt trends 1998–2003

	US	UK	Australia	Japan	Germany	Canada
5-year change	52.0%	63.0%	90.5%	7.6%	13.2%	31.3%
% p.a.	8.8%	10.2%	13.8%	1.5%	2.5%	5.6%
Ratio to income* 1998	113.0	120.0	115.0	133.0	111.0	111.0
Ratio to income* 2003	132.0	152.0	159.0	137.0	111.0	112.0

*Disposable income, i.e. after taxes.

Source: OECD, National Statistics.

large mortgages to be able to afford today's high prices. Meanwhile, many others are taking advantage of higher prices to increase their existing mortgages, either to pay down debt or to finance major purchases.

In a rising market it is quite rational for individuals to increase their borrowing to finance buying a larger house for themselves or an investment property. There are huge gains to be made on the upside. Somebody who bought a house in Britain or Australia in the mid-1990s with an 80 percent mortgage could easily have seen a fivefold gain in the equity in their house. But of course, this is a geared investment. With an 80 percent mortgage, a 10 percent fall in price would cut their equity in half, while a 20 percent fall would wipe it out altogether. In the worst-case scenario, where house prices fell 30 percent or more, many homeowners would be pushed into "negative equity."

ARE BANKS OVERLENDING?

The amount of lending in the economy is determined by financial institutions, based on their assessment of the risk and profitability of the lending opportunities open to them. Overall lending is not controlled by the government. Once it was. And in some countries in the developing world it still is, with banks facing a myriad of controls on whom they can lend to and at what interest rates. But in advanced modern economies the banking system can lend as much as it wants to, subject only to having sufficient capital from shareholders and meeting the capital and regulatory requirements of the authorities.[1]

Some people argue that the system encourages too much lending.[2] In principle, however, if banks are to make profits and avoid going bust themselves, they have strong incentives not to overlend. Still, if banks relax their risk criteria even a little, lending will increase. Suppose that banks raise the proportion of their mortgage book provided at a risky 100 percent loan-to-value ratio from 1 percent to 2 percent. If the risk of loss on such loans is seen as 5 percent (relatively high for mortgages), this may still be an acceptable risk/reward for the bank and be prudent enough for the regulators. But it is extra fuel for the market, allowing some people to buy who otherwise might not have been able to afford to do so.

Banks also make mistakes. During a bubble, bank managements can be caught up in the general euphoria. There is a danger, too, that the managements of banks are prepared to take more risks than would be ideal for their shareholders. If all goes well they earn nice salaries and large bonuses, while if the worst happens they find another job. Bank managements (and shareholders) also know that there is a potential guarantor for the system, namely the government.

Governments everywhere provide some sort of guarantee to deposits, to guard against a repeat of those scenes from the 1930s when people queued all night outside banks to get their money out, hoping to beat everyone else. In the US every deposit up to $100,000 is 100 percent guaranteed, a generosity probably made necessary by the widespread bank runs of the 1930s. Wealthy people now simply put $100,000 into lots of different banks and are completely secure. In other countries the system is less comprehensive. In Britain a Deposit Protection Fund, funded by banks, will pay 90 percent of any losses but only up to a maximum of £18,000 per individual, so it is no good putting £20,000 into several different banks. However, in addition to these explicit guarantees, most people believe that there are large banks that are "too big to fail."

The important thing about guarantees, both explicit and expected, is that most ordinary depositors pay no attention to what the bank is doing on the lending side. As a result, there is no real weight of public opinion pressing banks to be careful. Indeed, the weight of public opinion may be that it wants more loans. Fortunately, in the wholesale market other banks are paying attention and may show an unwillingness to lend to particular banks if they are perceived as following unduly risky practices. Such banks will therefore have to pay more for their wholesale money (a problem periodically faced by Japanese banks in the 1990s until the government explicitly guaranteed all deposits) or make every effort to find extra retail money, which usually means paying higher rates than other banks. The small investor should be wary of banks offering particularly high interest rates, especially if the bank itself is small.

The Basle capital requirements, introduced in the 1980s, were designed to reduce the risk of bank insolvencies. The Basle rules (already mentioned in Chapter 3) require banks to hold certain levels of capital against loans, with differing amounts of capital required against different levels of risk in lending. There are plans to develop this system further with the so-called Basle 2 system, but this is still under discussion at present and now looks unlikely to be implemented until late this decade.[3]

At present banks regard consumer lending in general and mortgage lending in particular as one of the most profitable areas of business. And lower interest rates have made it possible for people to fund larger loans. But when mortgages are agreed based on the appraised value of a house, while the value of housing is pushed higher by the easy availability of mortgages, there is a serious risk that house prices can reach extreme levels.

ONEROUS DEBTS

If house prices should fall significantly, people who buy near the peak with high loan-to-value ratios will face significant losses. High debt burdens can then exacerbate the impact of falling house prices on the economy as a whole. Just as rising house prices have encouraged strong consumer spending, so falling house prices could have the opposite effect. In the extreme case, we could see debt deflation, where people are forced to sell their homes to pay off debts, leading to further falls in house prices.

In practice, debt deflation in owner-occupied housing is rarely a widespread problem. Even in Hong Kong, where property prices fell 65 percent between 1997 and 2003, comparatively few owners sold in distress. People need somewhere to live, so they keep paying the mortgage, even though it becomes larger than the house's value. If they walk away they either have to pay rent somewhere else or live with relatives. Usually only people who really cannot afford to pay, typically if they become unemployed for an extended period, choose this option. Banks are reluctant to chase people who simply mail in the keys, partly because of the potential bad publicity but mainly because they recognize that most defaulters have no money. Nevertheless, they are entitled to do so and, fearful of legal action, people who still have a job or other assets just stay put.

However, this does not mean that house prices will not fall. Even a few distress sellers can give the market a downward bias. There are also new houses being completed and developers usually must sell for whatever they can get. Once the market is falling, other potential buyers become reluctant to take on a huge new commitment. So first-time buyers hold back, staying in shared accommodation with their parents or friends. And those thinking of trading up hesitate. Soon supply exceeds demand and prices fall further.

Of course, much depends on people's expectations at this point. Sometimes a small fall in the market can bring in new buyers, pleased to buy at lower prices. Thus a major housing bust is only likely if the whole economy is struggling at the same time and people are pessimistic about jobs and incomes. The psychology of the bubble goes into reverse and people focus on valuations again.

When house prices fall significantly, homeowners face the depressing fact that, even if they pay off their mortgage over time, the value of their asset has fallen. The good news is that since a house price decline will most likely be amid a general economic downturn, mortgage interest rates would fall substantially as a result. British and Australian mortgages are keyed off short-term rates, so with the floor to official short-term rates at zero, mortgage rates could go as low as 1.5–2 percent in a severe downturn.

In the US most mortgages are keyed off long-term bond yields, which would be unlikely to fall below 1 percent. This points to a rock-bottom mortgage rate of 2.5–3 percent, though with the caveat mentioned in the last chapter that mortgage spreads could rise in a crisis. Still, a sharp fall in mortgage rates would significantly reduce the pain of servicing the debt for homeowners and investors.

However, this would not alter the fact that wealth would be reduced. Moreover, in such an environment overall inflation is likely to be very low, perhaps negative, and this would mean that the chances of house prices recovering in a short time would be small. A fall of 20–30 percent in house prices could, in an era of very low inflation or even deflation, take 20 or 30 years to reverse.

For people who bought well before the peak and who keep their jobs, an environment of weak house prices is not a disaster. Five or ten or even twenty years later they might look back and see that trading up to a larger house was not a particularly good investment after all, but this realization might develop over a long period and perhaps not have much measurable impact. It could come as a shock, however, if they were assuming that house prices would continue to rise at a rapid rate and that the house would substitute for their pension. Moreover, people who buy near the peak could find it difficult to move home because of the need to save up to pay off the negative equity. They could be stuck, unable to move and with a large debt to pay off.

Investors in rental property are also vulnerable. Provided that they can find a tenant, low interest rates would make it easy to pay the mortgage and they could simply sit there with an asset worth less than they paid. But they do have an incentive to get out early if they can—to mitigate their loss. Many people who have bought recently have done so primarily for capital gain, with rental yields relatively low. It is probable that the more geared they are—that is, the smaller the deposit they have put down to buy the property—the more likely they are to sell. This is partly because of the fear of facing huge and rising negative equity if prices start to fall, but it could also be caused by a much more short-term view of the market.

For example, investors with an 80 percent mortgage, sitting on a 10–20 percent gain in value, might be tempted to sell if house prices then started to fall. Even after the expenses of selling, they could still see a profit. Hence we should expect that the greater the proportion of investment property and also the higher the loan-to-value ratio investors have obtained, the more likely it is that a wave of selling in this sector of the market will have a big impact on the whole market. It could be the tail wagging the dog.

OFFSETS TO WEAKER CONSUMER SPENDING

In the last few years the combination of rising house prices and growing borrowing has supported a low savings rate and high consumer spending growth. If this goes into reverse we can expect the savings rate to rise and consumer spending growth to become very sluggish. Instead of growing ahead of incomes, it would grow more slowly. For the economy to continue to perform well in these circumstances, another sector of the economy would have to do well. Exports, investment, or government spending would need to be leading the way.

Few countries have room now for rapid growth of government spending. Budget deficits are already too high. Strong investment in a period of weak consumer spending also might be unlikely. And this raises the risk that investment growth will slow and, consequently, productivity growth will ease back. The rapid growth of productivity in recent years has been a crucial component in the US success story. Not only has it underpinned rapid economic growth, enabling strong personal and corporate earnings, it has also helped keep inflation at bay. A slowdown in productivity growth would reverse some of these benefits and also make monetary policy more difficult.

That leaves export growth. Intriguingly, the US, the UK, and Australia all have a safety valve here because they have relatively strong exchange rates. In the event of a sharp slowdown in consumer spending, we should expect their currencies to fall to very low levels against European and Asian currencies, and their exports to grow more strongly. All three countries have current account deficits, the US and Australia at about 5 percent of GDP and Britain at about 3 percent of GDP, so this could be the long-awaited signal for a correction of these deficits. However, it would be crucial that domestic demand in Asia and Europe was strong enough to absorb the exports.

An important point to note is that a slowdown in consumer spending growth and a rise in the savings rate are not necessarily dependent on an outright fall in house prices. Even if house prices simply trend sideways for a prolonged period, as some expect, over time borrowing and mortgage equity withdrawal would slow and consumer spending would ease back. Undoubtedly, this outcome would be better than an outright fall in house prices, from the point of view of monetary policy makers, because the process would be more gradual. But it would not alter the fact that exports and/or investment would need to take over as the engines of growth.

THE BRITISH DILEMMA

The Bank of England has been wrestling with the issue of rising house prices and swelling personal debt for some time. During 2001–3, with the world economy weak and the pound strong, hurting exports and depressing Britain's manufacturing sector, the overall economy grew slower than its trend rate (around 2.5 percent) and inflation was below target. As a result, interest rates were cut from 6 percent to 3.5 percent, well below "neutral" levels. But with unemployment stable and consumers less pessimistic than manufacturers, house prices boomed.

The housing bubble threatens a weak economy in future if house prices fall abruptly, which could pull inflation below the Bank of England's 2 percent target. But trying to prick the bubble to avoid this risk might simply precipitate the crisis earlier. In 2003–4, with the economy strengthening, rates began to move up, but this was no more than the conventional monetary policy response, aimed at returning interest rates gradually toward the neutral level, believed to be around 5 percent in the UK.

The main reason for gradualism is that the Bank of England wants growth to exceed trend for a while, to help push inflation back up to the 2 percent target. But, perhaps inevitably, house prices and debt responded to this very gradual approach by accelerating in the first half of 2004. As already noted, the Governor of the Bank of England began to issue public warnings about house prices in mid-2004. In Australia house prices came off the boil earlier in 2004 in response to the combination of higher rates and public warnings, so the Bank of England will be hoping for the same result.

In the Britain of the 1980s, with inflation running at 5 percent or more, it was not uncommon to see rises in interest rates of 1 or 2 percent in one go and cumulative increases of 6–7 percent or more. Between 1987 and 1990 British interest rates were raised by 7.5 percentage points to head off rising inflation, and banks adjusted standard mortgage rates up from about 10 percent to about 15 percent. The result was a sharp economic slowdown in 1989–90 and a collapse of the 1980s housing bubble.

In 2004 tightening is aimed only at moving interest rates toward neutral and rate rises are likely to be ¼ percent or occasionally ½ percent. However, if growth remains strong and inflation accelerates above the 2 percent target, then a full tightening cycle over the next few years could take base rates all the way from 3.5 percent in 2003 to around 6.0 percent, in order to slow the economy. As a result, standard variable mortgage rates would rise from about 5 percent to 7.5 percent. In percentage terms mortgage interest payments would rise by about 50 percent, the same as in the 1980s, though in money terms the extra amount is only half as much as in the 1980s.[4]

At first sight this is reassuring. It would appear that a plausible interest rate shock would have half the effect it did in the late 1980s. However, this may be unduly sanguine. For one thing, in the late 1980s some of that increase in mortgage interest rates could still be set against tax, depending on the size of the mortgage. The limit was £30,000, which may not sound like much until you realize that the average house price in Britain in 1988 was only £55,000, so the bulk of mortgage interest would have been covered.

Moreover, a crucial difference is that household debt is much larger now and therefore the potential impact on incomes is correspondingly greater. In the late 1980s household debt was about 120 percent of incomes. Now it is well over 150 percent and rising. A given rise in interest rates now has a 25 percent larger effect than before (150 percent divided by 120 percent). Overall then, the 2.5 percent increase in interest rates that we could see now in a plausible tightening cycle would still probably have a smaller impact than the massive increase in the late 1980s, but the difference is less than it would at first appear. According to the Bank of England, *total* debt servicing costs (including principal repayments on mortgages) stood at just over 10 percent of incomes in early 2004, but are set to rise to around 14 percent in the next few years as interest rates rise, close to the 1990 peak of just under 16 percent.[5]

Perhaps the Monetary Policy Committee will continue to get it just right and keep the economy on a smooth growth track. However, the combination of the rise in debt and the housing bubble means that there is a greater than usual chance of a monetary policy mistake. The

Committee may try to inch rates up by a quarter point at a time, ready to stop tightening or even cut them again if house prices falter. But it could easily overdo it, because of the lags involved in the household response to higher interest rates. Or it could find that nothing happens to restrain the economy at first (especially likely if it takes a very softly-softly approach), and then suddenly one particular small rise triggers a big change in expectations and the economy and house prices turn around and head downward. Another possibility is that, in being careful to avoid a house price bust, it does not do enough and inflation is allowed to pick up in a serious way. This would almost certainly trigger yet more rate rises until eventually the economy and house prices turned down.

At that point, of course, interest rates would likely be cut, as they were in 2001–3. Then house prices surged in response, so could that happen a second time? If it did, once again a central bank would be relying on bubbling asset prices to boost the economy. Nevertheless, it seems unlikely that it would work the same way in 2005–6. For one thing house valuations are much higher now than in 2001. In London they were already elevated in 2001 and London prices rose much less than the rest of the country, while prices surged elsewhere. But now valuations are stretched everywhere.

Unfortunately, the monetary policy alternatives are not very attractive. Raising rates more sharply to prick the bubble and discourage borrowing could provoke the sharp economic slowdown that everybody wants to avoid. Moreover, unless or until inflation takes off, it would explicitly contravene the Bank of England's mandate to keep inflation close to 2 percent, neither above nor below. It is difficult to avoid the conclusion that the housing bubble really is out of control. It is going to be very difficult to manage a soft landing.

US BORROWING AND MONETARY POLICY

US household debt payments as a percent of income reached their highest ever level in 2000 at over 13 percent (see Chart 8.1). But, despite the fall in interest rates, the ratio has remained about the same level since then, due to increased borrowing. In contrast, during the early

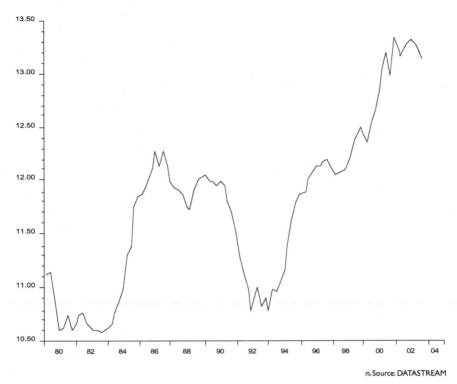

ຣ.Source: DATASTREAM

Chart 8.1
US: Household debt payments/income %

1990s in the last recession, the ratio came down sharply, with lower interest rates and slower borrowing.

As in the UK, part of the borrowing is linked to higher mortgages and rising house prices and part reflects rises in other debts, linked to lower interest rates and also easier borrowing terms. Nevertheless, given the current high levels of personal wealth in the economy and with unemployment in the 5–6 percent range close to the average for the last 10 years, it can certainly be argued that US debt levels are not excessive.[6] However, this assessment depends crucially on asset prices holding up and interest rates not rising too fast from here.

In Britain, when interest rates go up, virtually all homeowners face a rise in their monthly mortgage payment because of the prevalence of variable-rate mortgages. In contrast, fixed-rate mortgages in the US mean that rising rates mainly affect people looking for a new mortgage, generally first-time buyers or people trading up. They do have another effect

117

though, which is to make refinancing much less attractive, and this can reduce the amount of mortgage equity withdrawal. Overall, however, we should expect US households to be less sensitive to rising interest rates than British householders.

From the low point of 1 percent in 2003 the Federal Funds rate will first move back to neutral levels and then rise higher if the Fed needs to slow the economy at some stage. Bond yields will naturally be well above 2002–3 levels of around 4 percent, increasing mortgage rates on new loans. We might imagine a "neutral" level of 10-year government bond yields to be around 5–5.5 percent, which would imply mortgage rates of about 6.5–7 percent. However, if inflation threatened to accelerate and short-term interest rates were raised above neutral, bond yields and mortgage rates could go higher.

As in the UK, therefore, much depends on whether and how fast inflation reemerges. In the first half of 2004 core consumer price inflation jumped sharply higher, from below 1 percent in 2003 to just under 2 percent. This level is acceptable, perhaps even desirable, but concerns would grow if inflation moved up through 2 percent and looked like heading toward 3 percent. But unlike the UK, short-term interest rates are substantially below neutral levels, not just modestly. Hence the process of normalizing interest rates may be a tricky one.

A major surge in inflation looks unlikely, until late 2005 at the earliest. Unemployment remains well above the lows of the last cycle and the economy has considerable spare capacity. Estimates of the "output gap" (the gap between actual and potential output) are mostly in the 1–2 percent range, suggesting that the economy would need to grow 1 percent above its trend rate throughout 2004–5 before there was a risk of overheating. And with productivity growing strongly, trend growth is now seen as 3–3.5 percent or more. So although interest rates are likely to move up, the need for a severe tightening cycle, taking interest rates above the neutral level, appears unlikely to emerge before 2006–7.

Some people believe that rates will stay fairly low, because they believe that inflation risks have, to all intents and purposes, gone away. Interestingly, there are two camps here, whose views on the US could hardly be farther apart. On one side there are super-pessimists, who believe that the US economy will not be able to sustain a strong enough upturn to keep economic growth above trend for long. Some of these pessimists believe that the 2003–4 upswing was a temporary bounce, generated by low interest rates and the fiscal deficit, and that it will not last. They are particularly worried about consumer debt and house prices and tend to believe that the balance of risks is still toward deflation rather than inflation.

On the other side are super-optimists, who believe that the US economy can grow strongly for several years and, because of structural changes, the inflation response will be muted. They focus on factors such as the rapid growth of productivity, cheap imports from China, highly competitive labor and product markets, and the relatively weak inflation response in the last economic upswing in the 1990s.

Either view could prove right. But there is also the possibility, not given much credence in recent years, that inflation was held down by special factors in the late 1990s—for example the Asian crisis, which cut import prices, and the strength of the dollar—so that it could prove surprisingly virulent in coming years. If so, Greenspan's low interest rate policy could be setting the economy up for a renewed inflation problem earlier than generally believed.

Much depends on the path of productivity growth. A key reason for low inflation in the late 1990s was that, although wages rose, productivity rose faster. Despite the weaker economy during 2001–3, productivity growth stayed strong and so, with wage growth slowing, unit labor costs actually fell. But it remains to be seen whether this very favorable trend will continue. Usually productivity growth slows down once an economic upswing matures and wages are already showing signs of picking up.

My hunch is that US house prices as well as household debt will continue to climb higher for a while. Bubble psychology seems to be taking hold and historical valuations are being ignored. Just as in the UK, this will raise the stakes in future years and increase the risk of an ugly recession at some point. In Chapters 11 and 12 we will return to the issue of how to deal with bubbles, from a government point of view and from an individual investor point of view. In the next two chapters we step back for a moment and look more closely at the psychology of bubbles and then at the question of valuations.

PART III

ORIGINS AND SOLUTIONS

9 THE PATHOLOGY OF BUBBLES

According to conventional finance theory, bubbles do not exist. Stocks, houses, and everything else are priced by markets that are "efficient" and are made up of rational, calculating investors. Since the existence of a bubble would imply that valuations have departed from fundamental rational values, they have no place in this view of the world. Many researchers who follow this line are prepared to accept that not all investors are rational all of the time. But they believe that even if there are irrational investors, so-called noise traders, there will be enough people focused on fundamental values to override them.

The claim that bubbles do not exist seems extraordinary to most market practitioners. Sometimes it is based on the argument that the high level of asset prices in a particular episode was justified by the fundamentals. We heard in Chapter 2, for example, of the study arguing that the US market in 1929 was undervalued at the time based on profit and dividend trends.[1] Another study found the same for the German stock market in 1927, when an alleged bubble was deliberately pricked by the authorities.[2] By implication, it was the authorities who were to blame for creating both the US and German crashes by trying to prick what they mistakenly viewed as a bubble.

Other authors have claimed that, though particular asset price booms turned out not to be justified in the end, the expectation was nevertheless reasonable at the time.[3] Closely linked to this analysis is the argument that even if it looks like a bubble afterwards, it could not definitely be defined as a bubble at the time. In other words, bubbles can only be identified after the event, when the bust occurs.

This view of markets is based on the "efficient markets hypothesis" (EMH) and is widely held in the academic world. Part of its appeal is that it ties in neatly with much of the rest of standard, neoclassical economic theory, which also assumes rational behavior by consumers and business people. If markets are always correctly priced, they are providing exactly the right signals to businesses on how to allocate resources. Most economists believe strongly in the market economy and so are reluctant to admit that markets can misbehave.

Mainstream economists and finance specialists also like the efficient markets hypothesis for another reason. It enables them to work with a theory of market pricing that is easy to use and provides clear justification for valuations. We will come back to this theory later because, in my view, it is broadly correct in its approach to how markets should be valued. The trouble is that *actual* valuations depart from these values at times.

Nevertheless, there is a paradox at the heart of the efficient markets hypothesis. It argues that, because markets are efficient, there is no easy money to be made by trying to beat the market. The best way to invest in stocks, then, is to buy index funds, since on average they will do no worse than actively managed funds. Indeed, because they have lower fees they will usually outperform the majority of managed funds over time, as is confirmed by performance tables. The paradox is that, if everybody believed this and everybody bought index funds, there would be nobody looking at fundamental valuations to make sure that the markets were efficient any more.

I have labored the point a little because it seems to me that vociferous proponents of the efficient markets hypothesis contributed to the 1990s stock bubble through their arguments. By claiming that the market is always "correct," that bubbles do not exist, and that stocks always outperform in the long run, these theoreticians helped to reduce the sense of risk in the market. For every analyst who warned about a possible bubble there were not only several arguing that "it was different this time" because of changes in the economy or in technology, but also there were these theoreticians in the background with their calming voices saying that the market could not be far out of line anyway.

Since 2001–2 and the collapse of the stocks bubble, the efficient markets hypothesis has been having a rough time. Some proponents still blame the Federal Reserve for mistakenly pricking the bubble. Others point to terrorism and the Iraq war as new developments that brought markets down. We have already considered the possibility of policy mistakes, particularly over-easy monetary policy, and will return to this theme. But many finance experts and investors are looking to other explanations, within the markets themselves. And there are broadly three areas of inquiry: behavioral finance, "rational speculation," and critical state theory.

These areas are not necessarily mutually exclusive. Indeed, the interaction between them and with monetary policy is part of the story. But they approach from different angles. And while the efficient markets hypothesis does have an enormous amount of academic backing, these new theories are well grounded too.

BEHAVIORAL FINANCE

Investors are people and people are sometimes irrational. This may seem obvious, though the efficient markets hypothesis assumes that people are fully rational, unaffected by emotions, and not influenced by other people. Of course, many commentators have long doubted this approach and the idea of the "madness of crowds" goes back hundreds of years.[4] But ingenious experiments in psychology, which form the basis of behavioral finance, have now proved conclusively that people do not always behave rationally when it comes to assessing risk and making investments. And nowhere is this more evident than during a bubble.

PROSPECT THEORY
One of the most interesting areas of research is prospect theory, which puts forward a framework for how people make decisions in reality, faced with risk and uncertainty. It turns out to be very far from the rational approach assumed in conventional theory. A key early finding was that people actually hate losses more than they love gains (in contrast to the "rational" investor, who is assumed to treat them equivalently). This discovery was made in a famous experiment first conducted by two Israeli economists, Kahneman and Tversky, in 1979 and reported in one of a series of papers that earned them Nobel Prizes in 2002.[5]

In the experiment people were offered the following choice of bets (or "prospects"). They could choose either a bet with an 80 percent chance of winning $4,000 and a 20 percent chance of winning nothing, or a bet with a 100 percent chance of receiving $3,000. Most subjects chose the 100 percent chance of winning $3,000, even though the mathematical expectation of the first choice is higher ($4,000 × 0.80 + $0 × 0.20 = $3,200). This is not irrational, of course. After all, "a bird in the hand is worth two in the bush." But look at what happened with the next prospect, offered to the same group of people.

They were given another choice: either a bet with an 80 percent chance of losing $4,000 and a 20 percent chance of losing nothing, or a bet with a 100 percent chance of losing $3,000. The subjects predominantly chose the first option, even though the mathematical expectation of losses was higher ($–4,000 × 0.80 – $0 × 0.20 = $–3,200). Evidently they wanted the chance to avoid losses altogether, even though that would have only a 20 percent probability.

Similar experiments have been conducted all over the world with broadly the same results and it is now well established that people, and investors, suffer from *loss aversion*, the idea that the mental penalty from a given loss is greater than the mental reward from a gain of the same size. Some studies have calculated that the mental reward/penalty tradeoff is equalized only if the financial gain is three times the loss.

At first sight, loss aversion is no help in explaining bubbles. Rather the reverse, in fact. If people are frightened of making losses, why would they buy stocks or houses or other assets when prices are high? However, what happens during a bubble is that people start to believe that losses are unlikely. They put their faith in ideas such as that stocks are always good for the long term or house prices never fall. And so the usual feelings of loss aversion, which help keep stock and house prices at normal levels, are suspended.

Prospect theory has found several other areas where people do not seem to behave rationally. For example, *mental accounting* or *framing* is the tendency of individuals to organize their world into separate mental accounts. Hence they may borrow at a high interest rate to finance buying a car while saving at lower interest rates for the future. This is not to deny that there may be liquidity reasons for borrowing even when they have some savings. But it can lead to irrational decisions.

One important aspect of mental framing is that people often regard recent gains as "play money." They feel happy to reinvest, even in high-risk areas, because they have not yet incorporated the gain into their sense of their wealth, so they will feel much less regret if they lose it. It is this tendency that explains why gamblers are much less upset at the end of an evening if they lose some earlier winnings than if they lose the money they went in with. Again, in a long bull market it is easy to see how investors could happily reinvest their gains.

ANCHORING

Behavioral finance has found that people often use "rules of thumb" to help them make decisions in an uncertain environment. For example, how do people decide what something is worth? One common approach is called *anchoring* and is the tendency for investors to believe that the initial level of a market (when they first invested) is a kind of anchor that will pull the market back.

Remarkably, this is not even a logical, conscious process. One famous experimental example of anchoring is the Genghis Khan date test. Most people have heard of Genghis Khan, the warrior emperor from Asia, but few have a very clear idea of when he lived. In the tests one group of people were asked simply to estimate the date of Genghis Khan's death and the answers ranged widely over the last 2,000 years, roughly evenly divided between the first and second millennia. Another group of people were asked to write down the last three digits of their phone number and then estimate the date of Genghis Khan's death. The simple fact of writing down the phone number was repeatedly found to have the effect of anchoring people's minds on a three-digit number and the subsequent estimates for the Khan's death tended to converge on the first millennium. (He actually died in 1227.)

Anchoring has also been found to affect valuations by experts. One experiment took groups of expert valuers to a house for sale, gave them 20 minutes to look around, and also gave them a pack including information about the house and others in the same area.[6] The same pack was given to both groups, except that the asking price of the property was different. The agents told that the asking price was $119,900 on average suggested that $111,454 should be achievable, while those told an asking price of $149,000 thought (on average) that $127,318 could be achieved. Clearly, the agents told the higher asking price felt that it was excessive, but they were apparently influenced by it and did not mark down their valuation nearly enough.

Anchoring usually works against bubbles by encouraging the early taking of profits, because investors cannot believe that the market can rise too much. But it also works alongside regret aversion in encouraging them to hold on to losses in the expectation of a recovery. So in normal times, anchoring probably provides the market with a degree of stability.

However, it may start to work differently once a bubble is firmly underway. In the middle to late stages of a bubble, people are often willing to buy stocks or a house even when they are expensive compared to historical averages, because the price has been at that high level long enough for it to seem normal and comfortable. For example, during 1998 the US NASDAQ index was very volatile in a range of about 1,400–2,000. This was already twice its level of 1995, just three years earlier, but in 1999, when interest rates had been cut and profits were strong, people began to buy again, believing that the 1998 level was a reasonable base. Because they were anchored around that level, when they felt optimistic or heard good news they were willing to invest further, even though the valuations on many shares were 50 or 60 times earnings or more (and many stocks had no earnings at all). This helps to explain a typical element in most bubbles: the long period of price appreciation ahead of the final stages of the bubble.

Anchoring may also work to make people believe that *returns* will continue on the recent trend. By 1998–9 US stocks had been delivering double-digit returns for years, well ahead of other investments. Rationally, we might expect that future returns would necessarily be lower than average. But anchoring helped to make people expect a continuation of these returns and surveys repeatedly showed that people were expecting continuing double-digit returns. The survey of US house price expectations in Chapter 5 revealed the same tendency.

So-called fools rallies may also be linked to anchoring. Fools rallies, common when bubbles finally go bust, occur when, following a significant decline from the peak, the market has another major rally toward that level before finally succumbing. For the US NASDAQ index this occurred in the summer of 2000 when, after falling from over 5,000 down to 3,200, the market rallied back to 4,200 before collapsing again to a low of around 1,200 in 2002.

OTHER TENDENCIES SUPPORTING BUBBLES

Several other mental proclivities support bubbles. For example, our brains are programmed to make us feel *overconfident*. Behavioral economists have shown this conclusively with quizzes involving a series of questions such as asking people to guess the length of the River Nile. Participants are asked to offer not a precise figure but a range in which they feel 90 percent confident. If someone does not have much idea, the safest way is to provide a very wide range, for example 500 to 10,000 miles. In practice, most people offer far too narrow a range and therefore are wrong far more than 10 percent of the time. Another example of overconfidence is surveys asking people whether they consider that their driving ability is average, above average, or below average. Far more people believe that they are above average than below average.

One aspect of overconfidence is a tendency to believe that history is irrelevant and no help as a guide to the future. This is linked to a human tendency toward historical determinism, which leads people, looking back at past episodes, to think that the outcome should have been predictable in advance. In other words, historical events tend to be seen as having an inevitable logic that either would or should have been obvious to people at the time. And of course, because of overconfidence, most people believe that they will be able to see trouble coming this time.[7]

Stock markets particularly lend themselves to this view because investors believe that they can sell at a moment's notice. It is much more difficult with housing because a sale takes time, perhaps considerable time. But on occasion even stocks can move too rapidly. The 1987 stock market crash shocked many investors because they were unable to sell when the market slumped, as their brokers' telephone lines were jammed. Electronic trading might mean that this scenario will never recur, though of course technology can fail too and is more likely to do so if trading volume is heavy. Also in extreme circumstances, like for example on September 11th, 2001, trading may be suspended.

But even without any technical constraint on selling, some of the behavioral characteristics already mentioned, such as loss aversion or mental framing, may also make it difficult in practice for investors to sell when a bubble begins to deflate. So when the market first begins to fall investors may stay in, waiting for a rebound. More broadly, regret aversion may come into play as investors are reluctant to admit that they have been investing at the top of a bubble. Anchoring will tend to mean that they do not believe that the correction will be all that great. They feel that they can live with a 10 percent or even 20 percent decline as it is happening and have not grasped the danger that after a bubble, there is a chance of a fall of 50 percent or sometimes more. In a sense, they are still anchored in a bubble mentality.

Most people also tend to be *overoptimistic*. And when we put together overoptimism and overconfidence in the context of a rising stock market, the combined result is a tendency not only to believe that the market can keep rising but that the investor is particularly good at picking the right stock or market. Add in anchoring, which can mean that people start to regard double-digit returns as normal, and a bubble mentality is easily established. Inflation can have a complicating influence here because people are not very good at thinking in "real" terms, the way economists do. They tend to see a 10 percent gain over one year as a 10 percent gain, whether inflation is running at 2 percent or 6 percent, when in reality 6 percent inflation halves the gain.

The *herd instinct* is another very familiar behavioral trait. However, it is not simply a tendency to conform to what everybody else is doing, it is also the way the debate about an issue is framed.[8] For professional investors there is a particular problem here, which helps to explain why many managers of mutual funds or insurance or pension funds often try to ride bubbles rather than taking a contrarian view. Even if they believe that the market is too high it is safer to go with the crowd, even if the market subsequently falls, than to go against the crowd. It is safer to be conventionally wrong than individually wrong.

Cognitive dissonance is the mental conflict that people experience when they are presented with evidence that their beliefs or assumptions are wrong. For example, one classic study found that, after choosing and buying a new car, purchasers selectively avoided reading advertisements for car models they did not choose and were attracted to advertisements for the car they chose.[9] This tendency probably also explains why most of us feel comfortable with a particular newspaper or columnist. We seek out views and opinions that reinforce our chosen view. In relation to bubbles, this may explain why people are often not interested, or may even be angry, when they hear warnings that markets are overvalued. Instead, they will focus on articles offering encouragement that shares or houses are not overvalued and could rise higher.

Another general trait that may play a large role in bubbles is *disaster myopia*, the tendency to ignore major negative events that have a low probability. If we started to think of all the terrible things that could happen, to ourselves or to our investments, we probably could not get out of bed in the morning, let alone buy risky stocks or take on a large mortgage to buy a new house. So the things that happen very rarely we tend to ignore altogether. In contrast, just after one of these rare disasters occurs we expect a new catastrophe around every corner, which is called *disaster magnification*. Both of these traits are linked to a tendency to extrapolate from the recent past, rather than to take a longer view of history or of risk probabilities.

All the human behaviors analyzed in behavioral finance are believed to have been acquired as an instinctive response by our ancestors through a process of natural selection. And in the case of disaster myopia we can perhaps speculate why, if we think of how early man might have dealt with the risk of predators. If he just stayed in his cave all day he might have been safe but, of course, would never have found food. On the other hand, it would have been difficult to leave his cave every morning if he was convinced that a lion or bear was just about to strike. So we can imagine that natural selection would favor the man who put out of his mind the most extreme events that might occur and headed outside with only a modicum of caution. By contrast, if he had recently seen one of his tribe taken by a lion, we can imagine that he would be much more fearful of that risk and would proceed with extreme caution.

Taken together, all the tendencies identified in behavioral finance severely dent the concept that markets are made up of intelligent, rational investors carefully weighing long-term valuations of stocks and houses against fundamentals such as profits and rents. Rather, it suggests that people are not strictly rational, are pushed and pulled by all sorts of instinctive behavior, and are likely to go with the herd.

However, there are also papers in the psychology literature proposing that some of these biases disappear when the experiment is changed so that the probabilities and issues are explained clearly enough to subjects.[10] I take some comfort from this observation, because it implies that greater investment education, about risks and rewards as well as the dangers of bubbles, could reap rewards. However, I do not think it invalidates the idea that, in practice, these biases play a significant role in investing. Moreover, we know that as bubbles develop, people who would not normally be investors are drawn into the market and, without the benefit of experience, are perhaps even more likely to bring with them their natural biases, rather than a rational assessment of risks.

"RATIONAL BUBBLES"

One major objection raised against the theories put forward in behavioral finance is that, if there are rational investors among all this irrational behavior, the rational investors will win out in the long run by making more money. So the smart money will eventually take over as all the losers withdraw. However, there may not be enough "smart" money to outweigh the "silly" money as the bubble inflates.

For example, some pension fund managers were nervous about the US and UK stock market boom as early as 1996 or 1997 and moved out. But as the markets went inexorably up, their clients lost patience and moved funds elsewhere. By 2002, after the market slump, those managers were vindicated, but it was too late. They had lost many or all of their clients, and in some cases they had lost their jobs. The trouble is that most professional managers are evaluated on a relatively short-term time horizon. Few managers are assessed over more than a year and many have to contend with quarterly evaluations.

This observation leads toward the theory of the "rational bubble." If enough investors do not have a long-term approach to the market, it may be rational for others to ignore fundamentals too. So the "smart" move may be to run with a bubble and aim to get out before it bursts. For investors it is hard to deny that this may be the optimal investment strategy, provided that they can manage the risk, which for the ordinary investor may be hard to achieve. But clearly, if most investors take this approach the market is certain to be a roller-coaster ride.

In fact, quite a number of professional managers have little choice but to stay fully invested unless they are absolutely convinced that the market is in a bear phase. For example, if the mandate from a pension fund (i.e., the agreed investment objective) is to achieve the same return as an index plus 3 percent per annum without taking the risk of being more than 3 percent on the downside, there is no room for holding lots of cash. Indeed, their job is to stay invested and try to beat the index by clever stock picking, not to judge the market's direction. Nevertheless, I suspect that probably only a minority of investors in the 1990s, whether professional or private, consciously thought that they were participating in a rational bubble, at least until quite late on. The dominant mantra was "buy and hold for the long term," a very different strategy.

CRITICAL STATE THEORY

Another set of theories that sheds some light on bubbles and crashes is the newly emerged critical state theory. It is also known as the theory of complex systems and of critical phenomena, or more popularly as "tipping," in the sense that one small event can tip the balance.[11] The literature uses complex mathematics. Try the log-periodic power laws (LPPL) of herding, for example. But the theory is applicable to any system involving large-scale collective behavior, from the human body to the earth and the universe to markets.

The idea is that processes unfold over time as variables feed back on one another; the whole thing is so complex that there is no simple model that can predict when it will suddenly reverse. For example, the bubble phase, which usually develops after a prolonged gradual rally, may reflect a few small factors that push the market on to a faster growth track. Then all the characteristics of our bubble checklist come into play, interacting to reinforce one another. The asset price growth itself stimulates the economy and so appears to further justify the paradigm shift. Meanwhile new borrowing, which seems to make sense of taking advantage of the investment opportunity, further bids up asset prices.[12]

An important insight of critical state theory is that while in retrospect it always seems that the crash is the extreme event and therefore people are baffled why it happens exactly when it does, the extreme event is really the bubble. Of course, if everybody realized that at the time, the bubble would not get any larger. But as long as they don't (perhaps because they are "anchored" at high values), the bubble can expand further. And it is the process of positive feedback between investors, the market, and the economy that drives it on to vulnerable levels.

The particular insight of the "tipping point" arises at the top of the bubble. According to the theory, it does not require a huge event to turn things around because, unseen by most people, the market has reached a "critical state" where even a small event can have huge consequences. It is the straw that breaks the camel's back. The exact moment when one straw is enough to change everything is, according to this theory, simply unobservable. Note that this view of how things happen is diametrically opposed to the widely held view of history described above, where people see events as not only inevitably determined but fairly easy to predict.

Switching metaphors, a simple example of this theory would be if someone trickled grains of sand one at a time onto a flat surface. A small mound would form and every so often there would be a significant landslide as the mound crumpled, just with the impact of one more grain. There would be a recognizable pattern of periodic landslides, some large and some small, but predicting which grain would cause a landslide would be impossible. So it is with markets, according to this view. A bubble will grow and grow but eventually it will become too large and pop.

According to critical state theory, we cannot know exactly how big the bubble will become, nor the event that will tip it, which helps explain why people are so surprised when bubbles burst. However, we can still assign probabilities to the risk of a bust, even if we cannot predict the timing.

One of the major contentions of this book is that bubbles can be identified and, more importantly, can be identified before they go bust. There is, however, a question as to whether they can be identified sufficiently early for the authorities to prevent them inflating too far, since there is no doubt that it can be dangerous to prick already inflated bubbles. Of course, from an individual investor's point of view it is still enormously helpful to spot bubbles at any stage before they burst, even only just before (indeed, perhaps especially just before). But I also think we can do better than that if we use a perspective based on a probability or risk approach.

For example, if a bubble is enormously inflated, we should hope to be able to say that there is a 90 percent chance that this is a bubble and it is in serious danger of going bust. At an earlier stage of the rise in prices we might be able to say that there is a 60 percent chance of a bubble here (already), although the overvaluation is not extreme. With this conceptual approach in mind, we leave open the possibility that it is not in fact a bubble after all and will turn out to be justified by events. But as individual investors, we can start to underweight this asset because of the risk of a major fall. And the authorities can begin to look at various aspects of policy, including interest rates and lending criteria, to consider whether some adjustment may be desirable.

Bubbles and crashes occur when asset prices move pathologically out of line with the fundamentals. In the stock markets there are normally plenty of investors paying close attention to valuations, particularly professional investors but by no means only them. They are continuously calculating dividend and earnings yields and other measures of valuation, comparing them to bond yields and short-term interest rates, and making adjustments to their portfolios between cash, bonds, and equities. Most are also watching the performance of the economy and profits growth, both at a macro level and for individual stocks. In fact, they are doing exactly what the efficient markets hypothesis would claim. And most of the time valuations stay within reasonable ranges.

But sometimes they don't. Behavioral finance has thrown up so many examples of irrationality that the efficient markets hypothesis is no longer credible as a description of the way markets behave all the time. The theory of rational bubbles suggests that even people who believe a market is in a bubble will not necessarily be sellers. And critical state theory underlies both theories, by showing how positive feedback can take a market to overvalued levels. If only markets could stay with reasonable valuations, we would all be on much more solid ground. But what do we mean by reasonable valuations?

10 VALUING MARKETS SENSIBLY

Bubbles arise when markets depart from reasonable valuation ranges. We cannot specify a precise level for where a market should be, because expectations for profits, rents, and inflation are constantly changing, while central banks move interest rates up and down. Every business cycle is different to its predecessors and there is constant structural change too. But I believe that we can suggest broad ranges that make sense based on fundamental factors and are likely to hold over the longer term.

When a market is near the center of the range we can be confident that it is reasonably valued, while if it is near the top of the range an element of caution is appropriate, which needs to be taken on board by investors, banks, and government regulators. And if the market is above the top of the range, it may be entering a bubble, which deserves urgent attention. Alternatively, if the market valuation is near to or below the bottom of the range, the market is cheap and investors have a great opportunity. For the stock market the best way to specify the ranges is in terms of price–earnings ratios, while for housing we can use the rental yield; that is, annual rent as a percentage of the house's value.

THE POWER OF MEAN REVERSION

These ranges are not intended to be used as short-term forecasts. Just because a market is at one end of the range or even outside it does not necessarily mean that it will soon move toward the opposite end. Markets will naturally move around the ranges in an unpredictable way, potentially staying at one end or another, or outside it, for lengthy periods. When times are good and interest rates low, valuations will likely be near the top of the range, as in mid-2004 for example. And when times are bad, for instance during the world wars or the inflation crisis of the 1970s, or after a major economic slump like the 1930s, valuations will be low. As the market swings back through the middle of the range toward the opposite end, there is a process known as "mean reversion." This simply means that there is some average or mean level for market valuations, and that a period of high valuation is likely eventually to give way to a period of low valuation.

Mean reversion occurs all the time in nature. For example, the air temperature in London moves up month by month from February to August, but then falls for the following six months, cycling around its average temperature for the year. Anybody who forecast in August that the temperature would continue to rise in following months, based on the upward trend in the spring and summer, would have a rude awakening as the fall and winter set in. The mean daily maximum temperature in London over the year is about 14 °C and the usual range is about 7–22 °C. When we are outside those ranges we know that we are in a freeze or a heatwave and we don't expect it to continue for long.

The mean can obviously change over time. The average temperature does vary a little from year to year in London and indeed there are signs that global warming is taking it up. But the change is small and relatively slow compared to the swings around the average, which I shall argue is also true of financial markets. We may believe that global warming is happening, but still we will not expect August temperatures to become the norm in January, at least not any time soon. Of course, financial cycles don't have the same regularity as annual weather cycles. But the existence of mean reversion in financial markets is well established in the finance literature. The fall in stock markets in recent years looks like a classic case and there are plenty of other examples in history, including housing markets.[1]

The US stock market has had an average (or mean) price–earnings ratio of 14.6 times earnings over the very long term, according to Robert Shiller.[2] And the market has spent more than 90 of the last 100 years at a price–earnings ratio between 10 and 20 times historical earnings.

The last time it fell below the lower end of the range was in the second half of the 1970s, when the world economic outlook was threatened by simultaneous inflation and recession. But the early 1980s, when the PE ratio was as low as 8 times in the US (and also in Europe), turned out to be the greatest buying opportunity for investors in the twentieth century. Equally, when the PE ratio has moved above the 20 times level during the bubbles of 1929, 1987, and the late 1990s, sharp reversals have ensued.[3]

Because mean reversion does not happen quickly or predictably many investors ignore it, unwilling to wait for the eventual reversal. Instead, they try to ride the cycle and hope to get out at the top. They may also be reluctant to buy when the market becomes cheap, believing that it will become still cheaper and preferring to wait until the trough has clearly passed. The effect of this strategy is to exaggerate the cycle, taking the swings up and down further from the average. Winners may indeed be able to get out at the top, but others ride painfully down the other side. And some people are only sucked in at the top or sell out at the bottom.

Mean reversion in the stock market from an overvalued level can take place through a static market with a rise in company earnings, through a sharp market correction, or through some combination of the two. But the larger the bubble, the more likely it is that the adjustment will come from a sharp decline. When stock markets stood at 30 times earnings in 1999–2000, a correction to the average 14.6 times earnings would have required at least 10 years of normal earnings growth while the market "moved sideways." Since large bubbles involve a great deal of speculation the market is much more likely to tip over on its own, as speculators realize that they will not be able to sell on at a still higher price.

Mean reversion in property can be observed by looking at rental yields. Yields on prime London flats, for example, have generally ranged between 6 and 9 percent per annum over the long term. They moved higher than that in the early 1990s when the property sector was depressed by negative equity and the financial sector, London's main economic growth driver, was still weak. And the rapid rise in prices drove yields lower than that in the last five years, down to about 4 percent by 2001, though this seems unsustainable. Mean reversion on this measure could occur either by falls in property prices or by rises in rents. Over time rents probably will rise, as salaries trend up. But if rents stay in line with salaries and salaries continue to rise at 3–4 percent per annum, to move the rental yield from 4 to 6 percent (requiring a 50 percent rise in rents) would take 10 years or more. Alternatively, rental yields could move from 4 to 6 percent with a 33 percent fall in capital values while rents in money terms stayed the same. Mean reversion in house prices can also be seen in the cycles in the house price–income ratio for both Britain and the US, as noted in Chapters 6 and 7.

The process of mean reversion from an overvalued level can be terrifying to participants and often leads to a cumulative process that takes the market well below the mean. Of course, if this did not happen and the market did not dip under its historical mean level eventually, then the mean would move up over time. If the historical mean is calculated over 100 years of data, the upward trend would be very slow. But if the mean is computed over a shorter period, for example 20 years, it could move up smartly in a bull market.

Nevertheless, why shouldn't the mean value change? Don't markets and circumstances alter? During the boom times this is precisely what optimists argue, as has been repeatedly documented in studies of bubbles. In the late 1990s the case was made that the price–earnings ratio could easily go to 50 or above, implying a Dow Jones level of 30,000, because it is much easier to hold a well-diversified portfolio now than in the past and the risks on such a portfolio should be quite low.[4] Or, in relation to housing markets now, the low level of real interest rates combined with arguments about rising demand for housing are used as justification for expecting continued capital growth that therefore justifies a low rental yield.

Such arguments usually contain elements of truth and thus can seem highly plausible. And changing circumstances often can move the appropriate valuation on a particular sector of the stock market or a part of the housing market for a prolonged period. However, the broader the market under consideration, the more likely it is that the old mean, in terms of valuation, will hold and the market will eventually revert to it. Moreover, even if the mean does move somewhat, the swings we usually observe are likely to be much greater than the movement in the mean. For example, it may well be that the mean price–earnings ratio for the period 2000–50 will turn out to be higher than for the 1900–2000 period. But I would be very surprised if it moved up to more than 17–18 times earnings at most. So we can still be confident that we are in a bubble if we see a ratio of 25 times or more and we should start to be concerned at over 20 times.

MEAN REVERSION IS NO ACCIDENT

A crucial part of my argument is that mean reversion is not an accident. It is not caused simply by investors having alternate waves of optimism and pessimism. Rather, I argue that the mean value makes sense. And not only that, it is rooted in finance theory. Or put another way, there are good reasons for thinking that the mean does reflect the long-term value of that asset based on risks and returns. And those risks and returns are generated by fundamental trends in the economy, including economic growth, profits, the business cycle, and competitive pressures. Some movement around the mean is natural as investors reassess risks and returns and interest rates change. But when investors take markets a long way from the mean, they are moving away from fair valuations.

Finance theory has provided a clear framework for valuing different asset classes, such as bonds, stocks, and property.[5] The basic idea is that the more risk investors take, the greater should be their expected return. After all, if the risk of buying a particular asset is high, people would not do so unless they can hope for a higher return than with another asset. So we can build up a list of assets showing the long-term real returns that should reasonably be expected for each, ranging from index-linked government bonds (the lowest-risk asset) up through conventional bonds to stocks and property (see Table 10.1). The extra returns available on higher-risk assets come from "risk premiums." The risk premium for conventional government bonds covers the risk of inflation being higher than expected, while the risk premium for other assets covers risks such as bankruptcy, corporate bond defaults, rental voids, and market crashes.

Table 10.1
Reasonable return expectations

%	Normal real yield	Inflation compensation assumed 2%	Inflation risk premium	Credit/ market risk premium	Total return
Indexed bonds	2–3%	2% guaranteed	No risk	No risk	4–5%
Conventional bonds	2–3%	2% included in yield	0–1%	No risk	4–6%
Corporate bonds	2–3%	2% included in yield	0–1%	1.5–3.5%	5.5–7.5%
Stocks	2–3%	2% included in capital growth	Should move with inflation	3–5%	7–9%
Property	2–3%	2% included in capital growth	Should move with inflation	2–3%	6–8%

Notes: Each asset class needs to provide a 2–3 percent real return, plus 2 percent to compensate for inflation, assumed to be 2 percent per annum. An inflation risk premium is also necessary in the case of conventional government bonds and corporate bonds, since capital repayment will not move up if inflation is higher than expected. A further risk premium is required for investors to hold corporate bonds, stocks, and property, because of the risk of default, bankruptcy, or rental voids. The assiduous reader may have spotted that arithmetically the total return for corporate bonds and stocks could be as high as 9.5 percent and 10.5 percent respectively. I have capped the ranges at 7.5 percent and 9 percent respectively, because when market risk is high, real yields and inflation risk are usually low.
Source: Author's estimates.

These expected returns are based on the fundamentals of the economy. And we can link them back to market valuation measures such as the price–earnings ratio for stocks and the rental yield for property (see Table 10.2). We can also compare these expected returns to actual historical returns and I will argue that overall they are consistent, though admittedly there are some controversial issues. The most difficult factor to explain satisfactorily is why stocks seem to have provided better returns over the long term than the theory suggests, while government bonds have returned less than they should have. Various explanations for this have been put forward, none of which has received universal support. But I think that there is a plausible explanation for this discrepancy, to which I shall come in a moment.

Table 10.2
Reasonable returns, yields, and valuations

	Total return expected*	From capital gain	Yield, dividend yield, or net rental yield	Reasonable valuation range
Indexed bonds	4–5%	2% guaranteed	2–3%	2–3% yield
Conventional bonds	4–6%	0%	4–6%	4–6% yield
Corporate bonds	5.5–7.5%	0%	5.5–7.5%	5.5–7.5% yield
Stocks	7–9%	2.0–6.5%	2.5–5.0% dividend yield (incl. buybacks)	10–20 PE ratio (assumes 50% total payout)
Property	6–8%	2–4%	Net rental 2–6% yield	6–10% gross rental yield (assumes 4% costs)

*From Table 10.1.
Source: Author's estimates.

VALUING BONDS

The least risky long-term asset is inflation-indexed government bonds. The investor who buys TIPs in the US (Treasury Inflation Protected bonds) or index-linked gilts in the UK is not at risk from higher inflation or from private-sector credit risk. So there is no risk premium either for unexpected inflation or for default risk. Governments do default from time to time, particularly in emerging countries, the most recent case being Argentina in 2001. But the risk of the US or UK governments defaulting is very low and so we can look on these as the safest investments available.

Starting from these risk-free assets, we can ask what the characteristics are of other asset classes, such as conventional government bonds, corporate bonds, stocks, or property, in terms of return and risk. In what way do they involve greater risk and how much extra return does it make sense for them to offer? Let's start with conventional government bonds, for example the US Treasury benchmark 10-year bond. These instruments pay out a fixed coupon each year based on the face value of the bonds. At the end of 10 years the investor will receive back the face value of the bonds.

The risk with conventional bonds is that inflation suddenly takes off. Consider investors who invest $1,000 in 2004 into a US Treasury bond paying a coupon of 5 percent for 10 years. In 2014 they will receive their $1,000 back, but this will be worth less in real purchasing power if there is any inflation over the period. If the Federal Reserve succeeds in keeping inflation close to its (assumed) 2 percent per annum target, the $1,000 will be worth just under $800 in 2004 money. But the investors would probably be happy with this, because the 5 percent coupon more than compensates—the total payments they receive back over the life of the bond amount to $1,500. In fact, their real interest rate is 3 percent, a more or less average figure historically for real bond yields.

But now suppose for some reason that the Fed loses control of inflation and it averages 10 percent per annum. Now the $1,000 the investors receive back at the end of the 10 years would be worth only $386 in today's money and the 5 percent annual interest would not cover the effects of inflation. They would need to receive a total of $2,594 just to stay even with inflation and so their purchase of a bond will have turned out to be a terrible investment.

What do investors do about this risk? The answer is that the yield on conventional bonds has to offer a higher return than the yield on index-linked bonds. Otherwise, investors might as well buy indexed bonds and not have to worry about inflation. This difference is called the inflation risk premium. If the risk of inflation accelerating looks high, this premium will rise. And if it looks low, the premium will fall. In the current environment of low inflation and vigilant central banks, a reasonable range for the risk premium is between 0 and 1 percent.

Overall, the real return that governments pay to borrow using conventional bonds will normally be in the range of 2–4 percent and at least a little higher than the yield on indexed bonds, which has normally been in the range of 2–3 percent per annum. An important part of the argument in this chapter is that the market valuation ranges proposed make sense both from the investor's and the borrower's point of view. So for government bond yields it is important that the 2–4 percent real cost of borrowing is a reasonable long-term charge for governments to pay, because it is broadly in line with the performance of the economy. The numbers work fine here. In the US the long-run trend rate of growth has been in the range of 2.5–3.5 percent per annum, so over time tax revenues should be expected to rise at about that rate (in real terms). In other words, future tax revenues should be able to meet the servicing costs of that extra debt.

Another approach is to consider the nominal interest rate and compare it to the nominal growth of GDP. If nominal GDP rises at 5 percent per annum, comprised of (say) 3 percent growth and 2 percent inflation, then the government should be able comfortably to pay 4–6 percent interest on debt. Of course, if the government was paying 6 percent continuously, the top of my range, there would be a gradual deterioration in the fiscal accounts but, unless the government has an especially high level of debt, it would not be immediately crippling.

Overall then, real returns on government bonds in the 2–4 percent range seem to be about what we should expect. But now we come to a problem. Statisticians have calculated the return that investors have actually received on bonds historically and it turns out to have been significantly less. One of the most authoritative studies found that for the 100 years from 1900–2000, US bonds beat inflation by only 1.6 percent per annum, while UK bonds beat inflation by a paltry 1.3 percent per annum.[6] I believe the reason for this is simply that investors were caught out. They were buying bonds with the expectation that bond yields were higher than likely future inflation, but they were proved wrong. What caught them out was three major periods of inflation, including during the First World War, the Second World War, and then the wholly unexpected surge in inflation in the 1970s.

At any given time, investors were buying bonds in the expectation of returns in the 2–4 percent range, but they just kept being slammed.[7] Eventually, by the 1980s, they were deeply suspicious of governments and refused to buy bonds unless yields were very high in relation to inflation; that is, the risk premium was particularly high. When inflation unexpectedly came down fast through the efforts of Paul Volcker and Ronald Reagan in the US and Margaret Thatcher in Britain, investors were rewarded with huge gains. By 2003–4 it appeared that fears of inflation had, if not disappeared, at least been balanced by an equal fear of deflation. Perhaps finally, the bond market has recovered its balance and so my suggested range of 2–4 percent should be back on track.

PRIVATE-SECTOR BONDS

Now consider a more risky asset, private-sector bonds. These are bonds issued by private companies, so not only do investors face the inflation risk premium, they also need a risk premium against the danger that the company will go bankrupt. The yields on these bonds will therefore show a spread above government bonds based on the credit risk associated with that company. The shorter the time horizon the lower the spread normally, since it is easier to be comfortable that a company will not go bankrupt over a shorter period than over a longer period.

However, the spread varies with the economic cycle. For example, US bonds of BBB-rated borrowers (the lowest category of investment-grade companies) have mostly varied between 1.5 and 3.5 percent over Treasury yields.[8] Investors tend to be at their most pessimistic during recessions and their most optimistic during the upswing phase. Though bankruptcies can occur at any point in the cycle, they are much more common during and just after recessions and that is when the spread, or risk premium, tends to be nearer 3.5 percent, as for example in 1990 or 2001. During long expansion periods such as the 1990s, the spread has fallen to 1.5 percent or just below. At the time of writing the current spread is close to the average level of just over 2 percent, reflecting investor confidence in the economic recovery. In other words, investors are comfortable with an extra payment of 2 percent per annum compared with government bonds to compensate for the risk.

Does this square with historical experience? The US ratings agencies have been rating US corporate bonds for decades and have a long historical record of the probability of default in each rating category. For example, Standard and Poors data show that over the long term a portfolio of BBB-rated US corporate bonds has seen an average 5.3 percent of the bonds end in default over any 10-year period.[9] Usually in defaults not all the value is lost; that is, there is a certain recovery rate. If we take the recovery rate to be 25 percent (which is probably low), then at the end of the 10 years investors in a portfolio of bonds will receive back about $96 for every $100 invested. If they can buy the bonds when they are yielding 2 percent over Treasuries, they will have been paid handsomely for this loss, a total of 20 percent extra over a 10-year life.[10]

It would appear, then, that investors in corporate bonds are over-compensated for the risk, at least based on *average* data for the long period. The main reason for this is the danger that investors do not suffer only the average default rate of the last 10 years, but the worst case. Suppose they had bought in 1929, after which the bankruptcy rate for corporate bonds was exceptionally high. Then they would have lost much more than the average loss over the longer period.

In 2002 this risk was very much in investors' minds, with the danger of a double-dip US recession and possible deflation. There were also worries that the accounting irregularities discovered at companies such as Enron and WorldCom might turn out to be widespread. As a result, corporate bond spreads widened out dramatically. In 2003–4 the risk seemed to diminish with the economic recovery and spreads narrowed again. But investors are always conscious when they buy corporate bonds that the company could go bankrupt. And while the risk of a particularly bad 10-year period occurring again is low—the 1930s constituted by far the worst period in the twentieth century—there is no way of knowing for sure that it will not happen.

Can we relate the interest rate paid on corporate bonds to the performance of the economy as a whole? Over the long term, medium-risk corporate bonds are expected to show returns for investors of about 1.5–3.5 percent above government bonds, which suggests nominal yields of about 6–8 percent (including the expected inflation rate of 2 percent per annum). Since long-term borrowings like this will normally be for capital expenditure, for them to make sense companies need to be making a return on capital of more than the interest rate they are paying. This sounds about right. Returns on capital in the major countries on average are around 10 percent per annum. Overall then, yields on investment-grade corporate bonds of 6–8 percent make sense for investors and also for the companies that are borrowing.

THE EQUITY RISK PREMIUM

Now let's consider stocks by looking at the so-called equity risk premium (ERP), conventionally defined as the difference between the return on stocks and the return on government bonds. The ERP is one of the most closely studied issues in finance and remains controversial. There are good reasons for thinking that investing in stocks should earn more than investing in bonds. For a start, there is the bankruptcy risk on individual stocks, which is higher even than for corporate bonds because, in the event of bankruptcy, bondholders are paid ahead of shareholders. But stocks are also normally more volatile so that, even if they trend up over time, the investor could easily face a 10–20 percent dip in value one year, even without a major bear market.

However, I think the main reason for the equity risk premium is that historically there have been long bear markets in stock market history. For example, US stocks took 26 years to return to their 1929 levels in real terms. From the peak in 1968 they took 14 years in both the US and UK. More recently, the Japanese stock market today is still less than one third the value it reached in 1989.

The reason the ERP is controversial is that studies of historical data show that over the last 100 years investors in the US and UK have received close to 6–7 percent per annum in real returns from stocks and this seems to be too great when compared with the real return on bonds. UK stocks returned 5.8 percent above inflation, while US stocks returned 6.7 percent. In comparison, as we discussed above, the returns on government bonds were only 1.6 percent above inflation for the US and 1.3 percent for the UK.

The realized risk premiums therefore look surprisingly high, at 5.1 percent for the US and 4.5 percent for the UK. Academic studies assessing the size of the premium that ought to be necessary to convince investors to buy stocks rather than bonds, given the volatility of both, would suggest that the ERP should be closer to 3 percent.[11] One reason for this anomaly may be simply that the numbers are wrong. The figure calculated for the real return on stocks may be too high because of "survivor bias," the problem that companies that go bankrupt disappear from the indices. Indeed, in the twentieth century whole country markets have disappeared, for example Russia in 1917 or China in 1947, leaving investors holding stock certificates of value only as wallpaper.

But if we accept my argument above, that bond investors in fact got it wrong, the numbers still work out. All the time bond investors were expecting real returns of 2–4 percent, but they simply got zapped by inflation. With an expected real return of 2–4 percent on bonds, the extra return on stocks works out in the range of 1.8–4.7 percent for the two countries, clustering around the expected 3 percent.

With a return of 3 percent above government bonds and with government bonds themselves expected to return a real yield of 2–4 percent, this adds up to a total real return of 5–7 percent expected for equities. Add in 2 percent for inflation and stocks ought to provide a 7–9 percent nominal return. Again, as noted above in relation to corporate bonds, returns on capital are normally observed at around 10 percent, so this seems to make sense from the point of view of a company issuing new equity.

However, we can also look at it from the point of view of the likely growth of profits and dividends. Investors receive dividends. They may also get the benefit of share buybacks, which are essentially equivalent to dividends. And in addition, they will expect the company to grow and pay a larger dividend each year. Dividend yields historically are normally in the 2.5–5 percent range. In the US, share buybacks probably replace dividends for about 0.5–1 percent of this. The required growth in dividends to meet the expected return is therefore in the range of 2–6.5 percent. At 2 percent dividends would be growing only in line with inflation. At 6.5 percent real dividends would be growing at 4.5 percent, which is a very high rate to expect, though perhaps possible if economic growth is sufficiently strong. As we shall see later, at a 2.5 percent dividend yield the market is undoubtedly stretched.

There is one more arithmetical loop to make. The dividend yield combined with share buyback has to be paid out of earnings. So if the combined payout is to be about 2.5–5 percent of earnings normally and if the payout is about half of earnings, which is roughly the historical pattern over the long term, then the earnings yield (i.e., earnings as a percentage of the share price) should be in the 5–10 percent range. And the earnings yield is simply the inverse of the price–earnings ratio. So a 5 percent earnings yield is the same as a PE ratio of 20 and a 10 percent earnings yield is the same as a PE ratio of 20.

Hey presto. We have found a secure justification for the idea of the 10–20 times PE ratio as a reasonable range for valuations. If we go back to early 2000 at the height of the stock market bubble, none of the ratios made sense. The PE ratio stood at 30 times in the US and 28 times in the UK, implying an earnings yield of 3.3 and 3.6 percent respectively. Dividend yields stood at 2.4 percent for the UK and only 1 percent for the US, though we could add in stock buybacks to bring the US payout up to about 2 percent. But these numbers mean that investors had to be expecting dividends to grow by an extra 1–2 percent per annum over the long term compared to what would normally be likely, stretching plausibility to the limit. In other words, the stock market bubble was clear in the numbers.

An alternative way of expressing whether markets are low or high valued is in terms of the *expected* equity risk premium. We can say that at the height of the 1990s bubble the expected equity risk premium fell to an unusually low level, only 1–2 percent or less. In effect, investors temporarily forgot that, because of the risk in stocks, they should be pricing the market lower, so that it has more future upside.

There is a paradox here, because a low ERP means that investors are not expecting stocks to outperform bonds by very much. But in fact in a bubble people usually are expecting stocks to do well. Surveys during the late 1990s regularly reported that investors expected continued double-digit returns. The reverse is true at the end of a major bear market. Investors are so shaken by the fall in stocks that the PE ratio is low and, in effect, they are demanding an unusually high ERP to hold stocks. The paradox appears again in reverse. Nobody feels confident about stocks, so the equity risk premium is high, yet a high ERP can be interpreted as meaning that investors are expecting stocks to do much better than bonds.

VALUING PROPERTY

Finally, let's turn to the property market. We will look at it from the point of view of investors. What returns should they expect and therefore what is the risk premium on residential property? My guess is that a reasonable return should certainly be more than the 2–4 percent real return that we have specified for government bonds. Property is illiquid in comparison to bonds. Whereas a bond can be sold at a moment's notice, an individual property takes a considerable time, plus expense, to sell. Property of course has the advantage over bonds that it is protected from sudden inflation, since in general over the long term property prices are likely to keep pace with the overall price level. But unlike government bonds, where the face value will definitely be repaid on the bond's maturity, the price of property can actually fall. The coupon payment on government bonds can also be relied on, whereas property investors face the risk of a period of void when they cannot find a tenant. All this adds to the risk and makes property more risky. However, it is probably not quite as risky as equities. A company can go bust and be worth literally nothing, whereas a property nearly always has some value.

It seems to me, therefore, that property should be priced to return somewhere between government bonds and stocks and close to corporate bonds. We estimated that real returns on bonds should be about 2–4 percent per annum (including the inflation risk premium) and real returns on stocks should be about 5–7 percent. To squeeze in between these two asset classes implies that returns should be about 4–6 percent. Of course, the return to housing comes in the form of capital appreciation combined with the net rental yield. So we need to look at the likely capital growth over time in housing and then see what that would imply for the equilibrium rental yield.

Many private investors underestimate the ongoing costs associated with investment property. Professional managers usually expect annual costs to add up to around 3 percent of the value of the property, depending on its age and condition. This is made up of repairs, depreciation, finding tenants, managing the property, and insurance. On top of this there should be an allowance for voids. Buying and selling costs also need to be allowed for. Taxes and agents' fees mean that total buying and selling costs (in and out) usually amount to at least 5 percent of value and often much more. This means that with a 10-year investment, a further ½–1 percent per annum should strictly be added to the costs. Overall then, whatever the gross rental yield available, it is realistic to subtract costs of around 4 percent to obtain a net rental yield.

Over the long term, property values in a country as a whole tend to vary between keeping pace with inflation and growing at up to about 2 percent faster, depending on the flexibility of supply.[12] If we take the long-term expected growth in real house prices to be 0–2 percent per annum, and compare that with the 4–6 percent real return that we are looking for, then the net rental yield needs to be 2–6 percent. Adding 4 percent for costs implies that the gross rental yield should be in the 6–10 percent range. Somewhat higher figures should be expected for smaller properties in less good areas, where the various costs are likely to be greater than the 4 percent we have allowed, and also the risks of voids may be greater. Somewhat lower figures should be expected for larger properties in classier areas where maintenance costs will be lower.

Historically, gross yields normally have been in this sort of range. Currently, however, they are rather lower in many countries. We could say that investors are pricing housing on the basis that it is a low-risk investment. House prices are seen as something that will never go down in price for long, while investors do not expect to suffer long periods without tenants. But of course, a major part of the problem is that many people are expecting price growth far higher than the 2–4 percent nominal gains that I suggest here. So the risk premium is at historical lows and rental yields are below a safe range. At some point this market is likely to bite back.

A LOW-YIELD WORLD

The returns set out above are what a reasonable investor should expect over the long term based on an average inflation rate of 2 percent per annum. When market optimism is high, asset prices are bid up to high levels and yields are low. And when markets are pessimistic, asset prices are depressed and yields are high. So where are we today?

In the US today (mid-2004) indexed bond yields are at around 2 percent, the bottom of the range, and conventional government yields are at 4.5 percent, slightly up from the bottom. Earnings yields on stocks (the inverse of the price–earnings ratio) are just over 5 percent (PE ratio of 18–20 times), right at the top of the range. But rental yields for property are generally only in the 4–6 percent area, below the reasonable range. Admittedly data here are very imperfect but, as we saw in Chapter 7, other measures such as house price–earnings ratios also suggest a high level of valuation. Overall then, yields are generally on the low side (valuations high) and residential property in particular should be viewed with extreme caution.

Obviously, a key reason for these low yields is the low level of short-term interest rates set by the Fed. Disappointed by the low returns on deposits, investors have sought out alternatives, bidding up prices and pushing yields down. Low interest rates also encourage borrowing to buy assets. Of course, low interest rates are not the only requirement for low yields, otherwise Japan would have emerged from its 1990s stagnation far earlier. Confidence in the economy and in asset prices is also required.

The high level of confidence today is partly the result of the good performance of economies over the last 10–12 years. Countries where asset values appear particularly high, such as the UK, Australia, and Spain, have avoided a recession altogether in the last few years, while even in the US there has been only a relatively modest downturn, allied to unprecedented vigorous policy stimulus. However, there is another factor behind low yields, the remarkable disinflation over the last 20 years.

THE GREAT DISINFLATION

It is not an exaggeration to call the last two decades the Great Disinflation. Inflation reached unprecedented peacetime levels in the 1970s, peaking at over 10 percent in the US and around 30 percent in the UK.

Since 1980 it has receded to only 1–2 percent per annum almost everywhere and is at risk of declining to zero or beyond if the disinflation trend is not halted. Alongside lower inflation, interest rates have come down, both in nominal and real terms, and asset prices and wealth have risen to levels, relative to incomes or GDP, well above the average of the last 50 years in many countries. This is true notably of the US, where the fall in the stock market in 2000–2 has only dented wealth levels, still leaving them very high. And of course, the housing boom in the US, as well as in the UK, Australia, Spain, and elsewhere, has boosted wealth to high levels.

The beginning of disinflation coincided almost exactly with the start of the great bull market in stocks from 1982–2000. In early 1982 the price–earnings ratio stood at 8 times in the US, implying an earnings yield of over 12 percent. By the peak of the bull market in 2000 PE ratios had reached 30 times, for an earnings yield of just 3.3 percent.

It is eye-opening to decompose the gains in the markets due to valuation changes, versus gains reflecting real profits growth and inflation. The rise in the S&P 500 index was 1,265 percent from January 1982 to January 2000. But this reflected only a 104 percent rise in real profits and a 79 percent "compensation" for inflation. A full 383 percent of the rise was due to the higher PE ratio. Without the near quadrupling of valuations, the S&P index would have been at just 387 in January 2000 instead of 1,450.

HIGHER VALUATIONS

Why did lower inflation encourage higher valuations? There are several reasons, some valid, others questionable or even mistaken. A valid one is that lower inflation made it less likely that the central bank would jump on the economy again with higher interest rates. That meant that companies could enjoy a relatively long upswing, with rising profits. We have indeed seen longer economic upswings since 1982 and the high valuations in 2004 doubtless reflect hopes of another long upswing. If it lasts as long as the last two cycles, we could pencil in the next recession for 2009–10.

Another valid reason for higher valuations is that lower inflation has allowed real interest rates to come down. As already noted, bond market investors in the early 1980s demanded high yields to compensate for the risk of another sudden rise in inflation, keeping real yields unusually high. But gradually, as disinflation became part of the landscape, this inflation risk premium has been eroded. For a while in 2003 it seemed to disappear altogether as investors began to expect deflation.

For many investors, it is enough that lower deposit rates and lower bond yields make stocks more attractive in relative terms. A more technical perspective is to view the value of a company as being the sum of all its future profits, discounted to the present. And if the discount rate (i.e., the bond yield) is lower, then the value of the company is higher.

Another possible reason for higher stock valuations in a period of lower inflation is that there are good reasons for thinking that economic growth will be stronger. High inflation has the effect of making the price mechanism work less efficiently, as people find it hard to tell whether a price increase means higher demand for that good or is just general inflation. High inflation is also inefficient, in that firms have to keep altering their price lists and people may waste lots of time juggling their financial affairs. Low inflation takes away these inefficiencies and therefore should mean that the economy performs better.

As well as creating faster economic growth, low inflation may improve the quality of profits. Inventory management becomes less critical and genuine value-enhancing measures such as new investment and cost cutting may be given more weight. However this argument can be taken too far. Enthusiastic investors sometimes forget that increased economic efficiency will normally only temporarily boost profits. Eventually competitive pressures mean that increased efficiency flows through into higher consumer incomes through reduced prices.

All these factors do suggest that in a world of lower inflation, price–earnings multiples could reasonably be higher than in the 1970s world of high inflation. Nevertheless, it is sometimes argued that lower interest rates in themselves justify a higher price–earnings multiple. This argument is certainly wrong. If interest rates are lower because inflation is lower, then the effect should simply cancel out because forecasts of future profit growth must necessarily be lower too.

There is also a danger that investors are still thinking of investments as though we lived in a high inflation world and so, looking for double-digit returns, they buy stocks or mutual funds that have recently achieved those returns. The problem is that looking for double-digit returns in a period of low inflation is unrealistic, so that any stock or fund that is achieving such returns is probably either taking large risks or rapidly becoming expensive. During the 1970s when inflation was often 8–10 percent or more, double-digit returns were essential to avoid losing out in real terms. In a world where inflation is 2 percent per annum, returns of 5–6 percent are already good and higher returns are only possible by taking on much more risk. So in the 1990s, to the extent that investors were pouring money into stock market sectors or funds with a double-digit growth history, they may have been pushing valuations too high.

In a sense, we are talking here about a form of "inflation illusion." In the 1970s economists realized that many people were suffering from "money illusion." For example, people were pleased if they received a higher pay rise one year than the next, not taking into account that inflation was higher and therefore they were no better off. But now most people have grown up with inflation and expect that prices will always trend up. Money is not seen as a store of value in itself. So people are unimpressed by low returns and, alongside that, tend to expect that asset prices will trend higher at a fairly rapid rate. In short, they have the illusion that inflation is just an inevitable fact of life and that they should continue to expect prices to double every 15–20 years or so. In fact, at 2 percent inflation it takes 35 years for the price level to double and at 1 percent inflation it would take nearly a lifetime (about 70 years).

ECONOMIC UPSWINGS AND MARKET SETBACKS

One important effect of the general disinflationary trend, as already stated, is that economic upswings lasted longer after 1982 then before. The US and UK enjoyed upswings lasting ten years, while continental Europe saw an eight-year upswing. And this may be implicated in the higher incidence of bubbles. It is rare to see any kind of bubble very soon after a recession. There is normally too much caution around for people to take big risks. It is only after a few solid years of good growth and low unemployment that people start to relax and take on more risks, including borrowing to buy assets. And if asset prices start to rise and still the economy looks good, that is when there is a real danger of a bubble developing. It is as though asset markets lose touch with reality the longer the fun goes on, rather like children getting overexcited at a party.

As we saw, stock markets entered a bubble during 1987 but higher interest rates pricked it quickly and there was very little economic damage, with the help of a rapid reduction in interest rates immediately after the 1987 crash. Stocks then stayed at reasonable valuations for nearly 10 years, chastened perhaps by the crash and also by the economic slowdown in the early 1990s. But then, starting around 1996, after several years of the new expansion a bubbly atmosphere reemerged and this time it was allowed to let rip. Disinflation had been so successful that the central banks saw no risk of consumer price inflation and decided to ignore asset price inflation.

In the last few years, the world slowdown has meant that again, consumer price inflation is not a problem. In the US, consumer price inflation between 1 and 2 percent on the core index (excluding food and energy) is now seen as satisfactory. In the UK, inflation has remained below the Bank of England's target despite a relatively strong economy (compared to many other countries) and unusually low unemployment. In continental Europe, inflation stayed above the European Central Bank's target for a while, reflecting the lack of progress in reforming the labor market, but this did not prevent the ECB from cutting rates during 2001–3. Hence housing markets have been left to bubble away, without interruption.

If we continue to live in a world of modest inflation, long economic upswings with mild downturns, and limited political risks, perhaps yields can stay low. But there is a paradox here. If we believe that high investment and strong growth will be the trend in coming years, returns need to be reasonably high to stimulate that investment. But this would normally imply higher yields. In other words, there is a tendency (over the medium to long term) for strong economic growth to be associated with high returns and high real interest rates. It will defy the rules of economics if we can enjoy current relatively strong economic growth rates and relatively low real interest rates for long. Either growth will slow, affecting expectations for profits growth, or interest rates will rise.

Current low market yields therefore suggest a vulnerability to market setbacks. The normalization of interest rates over the next few years will present a challenge. However, any bad economic or political news could be especially difficult to absorb from low yield levels. An unexpected recession would be particularly damaging, not least because neither the Fed nor the government has any ammunition left for stimulating the economy. But so would a rise in interest rates above what is currently expected. It remains to be seen whether there is a path between slowdown and high interest rates that will provide sufficiently good news on profits combined with moderate interest rates.

Even if we avoid the worst scenario, the analysis of this chapter implies that investment returns will necessarily be lower in coming years, simply because we begin from low yields. For investors this may mean that returns will come more from picking the best stocks and from trading market cycles rather than from a buy-and-hold stance. A final implication is that if we do avoid bad news in the next two to three years, with values already high, watch out for more bubbles. Housing is already at risk, but stocks could bubble again too.

With the help of the ranges derived above, individuals can see when markets are expensive or cheap and perhaps avoid being caught up in bubbles. But these ranges can also serve as a guide to governments in dealing with asset bubbles and busts. In the next chapter we turn to what governments can do, both to control the growth of bubbles and to limit the impact of subsequent busts on the economy.

11 NEW POLICY APPROACHES

The central thesis of this book is that movements in asset prices are coming to dominate the performance of the economy. Yet asset prices are subject to bubbles and busts that can have a profound impact on the economy. Can governments do anything about this? And indeed, should they even try, or would they be in danger of making the problem worse?

In the last couple of decades good macroeconomic policy has come to be understood as controlling budget deficits while using interest rate policy to keep inflation low and stable. During the 1990s upswing the US government did a good job of moving the budget into surplus and bringing down government debt. Meanwhile, the Fed concentrated on controlling inflation and can reasonably claim that, with economic growth very strong while inflation stayed low, it too did a good job. But the two were unable to prevent the stock market bubble. And by cutting interest rates far and fast to limit the damage from the stock bust, they have created a housing bubble.

Policy in the UK has also conformed fairly closely to orthodox prescriptions. The large government deficit that resulted from the 1990 recession was eliminated by the late 1990s and, to many people's surprise, the new Labour Government took the budget all the way into surplus for a while, before eventually succumbing to the temptation to spend more money on health and education. Meanwhile, the Bank of England is widely perceived to have done an excellent job in managing interest rates and the economy. The UK avoided recession during the world downturn of 2001–3 while inflation stayed close to target. But again, the UK now faces a serious housing bubble.

Australia is a similar story. The Reserve Bank of Australia is rightly credited with skillful use of easy monetary policy in the late 1990s to navigate through the damaging effects of the Asian crisis on its economy. And like the UK, Australia also avoided recession in recent years, with the help of low interest rates. But home prices went into a bubble.

SHOULD GOVERNMENTS DO ANYTHING?

One view of asset price bubbles, which has strong support from many free market economists, is that governments should do nothing. Bubbles and busts are a normal feature of the market economy and people need to learn that. It is better to have a moderate bust now than to use monetary or other policies to prevent it and then face a larger crash later. Perhaps a bust will lead to a recession, but that will not last for ever and afterward investors will be more cautious about making the same mistake again, at least for a while.

On this view what is important is for the government to avoid, or at least to limit, "financial instability" following an asset price decline. The most dramatic kind of financial instability occurs when a major bank goes bust, triggering runs on other banks as depositors try to withdraw their money. Historically this has often caused economic crises because of the loss of confidence involved. But financial instability can also be more insidious. Instead of making front-page news it manifests as a lending strike by banks, a so-called credit crunch. Faced with worries over existing bad loans and concerned about the economic outlook, banks become reluctant to lend.

So according to this view, if stocks or housing fall sharply but banks are not severely affected, there is nothing too much to worry about. There may be wealth effects having an impact on the economy, but these can be counteracted by lower interest rates and easier fiscal policy. And if the banks *are* threatened by losses arising from the asset price bust, the answer is to ensure that the system is provided with enough liquidity to avoid a crisis and then to deal with the position of the specific banks affected. Generally, if a bank has lost more than its capital it will have to be closed or taken over by another bank or by the government. Shareholders lose money but depositors should be repaid, using taxpayers' money if necessary.

What about losses in other financial institutions? The legacy of the 1990s stock bubble has been felt mainly among insurance companies and pension funds, rather than banks. Market losses may well have wealth effects in the economy, but they are unlikely to threaten the whole system. For example, losses among insurance companies (as emerged in 2002 in the UK and Europe) may result in lower payouts on life policies or pensions. If someone's pension is reduced by 10–20 percent or even more, it is very bad news for them but not a general crisis. In contrast, allowing banks to go bust can threaten the whole payments system because everybody tries to take out their money at the same time and the system collapses. If the insurance companies themselves are threatened with becoming insolvent because they have fixed liabilities, then the government may have to ensure that they are recapitalized—probably by being taken over by another company. But an insurance company going bust does not in any case usually threaten the same systemic problems as a major bank going under, because it is not a key link in the payments system.

The "laissez faire" approach to bubbles is attractive in principle. Government attempts to control things usually end up in a morass of interest-group politics, distortions of the economy, and, quite frequently, corruption. However, there are serious objections in practice. First, central banks are already involved in asset prices because of their role in setting interest rates. Indeed, they may be part of the problem in the first place, in allowing or encouraging bubbles to develop. At times investors have seemed to take comfort from the belief that interest rate policy in fact does respond to asset prices, but only when they fall. This expectation (the "Greenspan put," as we saw in Chapter 3) may tend to encourage asset prices to rise higher than otherwise, threatening a larger fall.[1]

Secondly, bubbles normally do not develop without significant lending being involved, usually by banks. But governments are extensively involved in regulating and supervising banks, so they need to take asset prices into account in this process, not least because a bust in asset prices may threaten banks' solvency. Around the world, when banks fail on a large enough scale, threatening the system or wiping out the savings of significant numbers of people, governments nearly always end up having to contribute taxpayers' money to recapitalize them. So bubbles can bring a fiscal cost.

Thirdly, governments do have a responsibility for pension policies. Decisions have to be taken on what level of state pension is to be promised and how tax relief on pension contributions is to be given, to avoid taxing income twice. Governments could end up needing to put in taxpayers' money here too, if large numbers of corporate pension schemes fail.

Finally, and perhaps most importantly, when bubbles lead to booms and busts, the resulting economic instability can be very damaging. The economy may face either a serious recession and the risk of a debt deflation or, if there is an overenthusiastic attempt to kick-start the economy, a bout of inflation.

In my view, these reasons are sufficient to make it worth carefully considering what policy measures might be available. However, the skeptics regarding an active approach to asset prices raise two further problems. How can central banks deal with asset prices as well as discharging their primary responsibility to limit consumer price inflation? And how can governments know better than markets whether or not assets are sensibly valued?

ASSET PRICES AND MONETARY POLICY

It is interesting to compare the policy environment now with the situation in the late 1960s and early 1970s. At that time policy was still geared to the postwar Keynesian consensus view that active monetary and fiscal policy should focus primarily on avoiding high unemployment. However, inflation was gradually accelerating and a huge policy debate opened up between "Keynesians" and "Monetarists." The initial Keynesian solution was to combat inflation with income policies, without changing the rest of the approach. But incomes policies were dismal failures in most countries and had to be abandoned. Gradually, the old Keynesian consensus gave way to the current orthodoxy, which sees the level of unemployment as determined by structural factors over the long run and focuses monetary policy entirely on controlling inflation.

Now we face a new environment. While ordinary inflation has faded as a problem, asset price volatility and financial instability have emerged as major worries.[2] Yet conventional policy is still rooted in the anti-inflation orthodoxy of the last couple of decades, which takes very limited account of asset prices. Is it time for a new approach? In particular, is it time that central banks leaned harder against emerging bubbles?

Asset prices affect inflation and growth in various ways. If asset prices are high and rising, economic growth is likely to be well supported, which will eventually, when the job market becomes tight or capacity utilization rates rise particularly high, lead to higher inflation. There is therefore a clear case for higher interest rates when asset prices are surging and the economy is strong, even though current inflation may be well behaved. Similarly, if asset prices are falling and the economy is weak, cutting interest rates is the best antidote to both and a recovery in asset prices will help reinforce the economic recovery and vice versa. In these cases, then, there is no conflict between monetary policy aimed at managing inflation and policy aimed at controlling asset prices.

However, suppose inflation is at or below target and the economy is seen as either relatively weak or as growing satisfactorily, while asset prices are rising strongly. Then, conventional policy suggests that the central bank should ignore asset prices because raising interest rates might hurt the economy. This was the situation for the US economy in much of the 1990s.

In the 1990s the Fed almost certainly held interest rates too low overall. It is easy to be critical after the event, but many commentators argued the same at the time. The combination of a strong economy and soaring stock prices certainly pointed to the need for a more restrictive stance.[3] Moreover, the apparent increase in the trend rate of growth of the economy, from around 2.5 percent to 3.5 percent per annum, also pointed that way because of the implication that the "neutral" rate of interest should be higher.

A simple measure of the stance of policy is to subtract the growth of nominal GDP (including real growth and inflation) from the Federal Funds rate (see Chart 11.1). When the funds rate is below nominal GDP

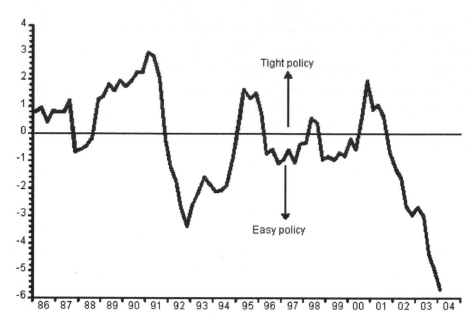

Source: DATASTREAM

Chart 11.1
Fed funds rate less nominal GDP growth

growth, we can say that policy is easy; when it is above, policy is tight. Overall, Fed policy was generally looser in the 1990s than in the 1980s. We can also see that policy since 2001 has been much looser than in the early 1990s. But I would focus the main criticism on policy in the period 1997–99.

The Fed's overstimulatory policy at that time was partly a response to two shocks. One was the near bankruptcy of the hedge fund Long Term Capital Management (LTCM) following the Russian default, in the autumn of 1998. This led to large-scale unwinding of bond positions and turbulence in the financial markets that threatened to hurt the economy, so the Fed was quite right to respond swiftly. But it was then slow to tighten monetary policy again in 1999, apparently because of fears of a shock from the Millennium Bug at the end of the year.

The risk of major problems with computers on January 1st, 2000 meant that the Fed had to be particularly careful to ensure ample liquidity for banks at the year end. But it has never been satisfactorily explained why the Fed felt it needed to dawdle in raising interest rates during 1999. The two issues are separate when the liquidity needs were only likely for a limited period. But the Federal funds rate was moved up only very cautiously in 1999, from 4.75 percent to 5.5 percent. This lapse encouraged a new inflation of the stocks bubble, with the S&P 500 index rising from 1,000 points after the slump in the autumn of 1998 to over 1,500 points in just 15 months.

The dilemma for the central bankers is that if a bubble grows large and then bursts, it may bring a serious recession, making it very likely that they will undershoot their inflation target in two or three years' time. But if they raise interest rates to stem the inflation of the bubble, unless the economy is strong they may kill the bubble and end up triggering the very problem they were trying to avoid. And of course, if the economy is indeed strong, higher interest rates may have little effect on the bubble at first, until suddenly there is a sharp swing in expectations. It is always hard to deflate a bubble gradually.

Central bankers are well aware of the problem and some are arguing that it may be desirable to "lean" more heavily against bubbles than Mr. Greenspan attempted to do in the 1990s. Sometimes this argument is couched, neatly within the prevailing orthodoxy, as a need not just to target inflation one or two years ahead, but to take a longer view.[4] This flexibility sounds like a step in the right direction, though it still leaves the same dilemma of what exactly is the right level of interest rates and how central bankers should explain why they want to raise them when inflation is still low. It also raises some disquiet over the balance of "rules versus discretion" for monetary policy. Rules that are simple, like "target 2 percent inflation in 24 months' time," are much more attractive than vague and potentially conflicting longer-term approaches.

One way to keep a strictly rules-based approach would be to include asset prices in the targeted measure of inflation.[5] In principle, this would remove the conflict by giving central bankers one target to hit with their one available instrument, interest rates. However, it is difficult to know which assets to include and what weight to give them. Moreover, the behavior of asset prices can be fundamentally different from the behavior of consumer prices, particularly during bubbles. So the idea has not gained much traction.

BUBBLE WARNINGS

While many central bankers are cautious about targeting asset prices, some are terrified even of drawing attention to bubbles. They fear that the markets will one day sell off sharply and they don't want to encourage that, either as a committee or as individuals. Instead, they are inclined to cross their fingers, hoping that perhaps the market does know something they don't or that it will deflate quietly in that usually elusive "soft landing."

Here again there is what I consider a legitimate criticism of Chairman Greenspan's policy in the 1990s. After his "irrational exuberance" speech in 1996, when the S&P 500 index stood at about 650, he dropped the issue even as stocks soared on up to 1,100 just before the LTCM crisis and then on up to the high above 1,500. He may have been scared of pricking the bubble, though his speeches before and since put more emphasis on the problem of knowing whether a market is in a bubble or not.

Of course, warnings may not have much effect. Mr. Greenspan's warning in 1996 certainly did not. And the Reserve Bank of Australia's repeated warnings about a house price bubble in 2002–3 also seemed to have only a limited impact. Warnings seem to need to be backed up with changes in interest rates or other policy measures. In late 2003 and early 2004, when the strength of the economy encouraged the Reserve Bank to push interest rates upward, the combination of warnings and higher rates began to cool the market. But by then the bubble was already well advanced. It will be interesting to see whether the Bank of England's warnings in mid-2004 have any effect, though of course they too are combined with rising rates.

As well as controlling inflation, central banks are often also responsible for overall financial stability, sometimes called macrostability or macroprudential to differentiate it from the separate role of supervising particular institutions (microprudential). Again though, the people responsible for financial stability may be reluctant to draw attention to bubbles. Hopefully, behind the scenes, they can influence banks to slow down their lending, a point to which we will return below. But investors cannot expect to hear strident warnings from this quarter either.

In recent years most countries have separated out financial regulation and supervision from the central bank function. And increasingly the trend is to fold the task of supervising and regulating all financial institutions such as banks, insurance companies, brokers, and so on into one institution, such as the Financial Services Authority (FSA) in the UK. The FSA of course has a profound interest in whether bubbles are developing, because bubbles might damage the institutions they are regulating. But again, if a bubble is already well advanced, regulators will be nervous about crying wolf too loudly, in case that precipitates a crisis.

Governments have even less interest in drawing attention to the dangers of asset bubbles. Voters generally like bubbles. Many people profit from them, though for some the gains turn out to be only on paper and disappear later. It is true that there is sometimes resentment of the get-rich-quick windfalls of early investors and heavy speculators, but the sense of revulsion against speculators and markets mostly occurs after a bubble has burst, not before. Housing bubbles also have their opponents, because young people may be priced out of the market and poorer people and those in social housing miss out on the gains. But in general, it is easy to win elections during bubble periods, because people feel wealthy and the economy is doing well.

This discussion of the dilemma facing the monetary and financial stability authorities leads to three conclusions. First, it would be much better if we could identify asset market misalignments early, before they have become major bubbles. Secondly, this identification may need to be done by independent experts since central bankers, regulators, and government ministries, not to mention industry insiders, will generally be reluctant to point to bubbles. Thirdly, we need to find other means of controlling bubbles rather than relying purely on interest rates, since monetary policy objectives sometimes conflict.

AN ASSET VALUATION COMMITTEE

To tackle the first two points, in 2002 I proposed the setting up of an Asset Valuation Committee or AVC.[6] The idea is to establish an experienced group of financial experts to study fundamental trends in stock and property prices and identify reasonable long-term valuation ranges. The committee could include a mix of central bankers, academics, and financial practitioners. If and when it judged asset prices were moving out of these ranges, it could issue public warnings for investors, lenders, and policy makers. It could use a system of amber and red alerts or, better still, a graduated scale to signal the risk. In 2003 a similar idea was put forward, proposing a committee that would regularly publish a "speculometer," a measure of the degree of speculation in the market.[7]

My suggestion is that the AVC should be an independent part of the central bank, rather like the FOMC in the US or the Monetary Policy Committee of the Bank of England. But some people argue that any such committee would be better if it were outside the government altogether. One possible model is the Shadow Open Market Committee, a group of academic monetary economists in the US that makes recommendations for US interest rates, in effect shadowing the activity of the FOMC. Similar committees exist in Europe to shadow the European Central Bank and the Bank of England. However, I suspect that an official committee, separate from monetary policy making but inside the central bank, would have much more impact on market expectations.

Overvaluations are usually only widely recognized when they have already reached dangerous proportions. It may well be too late to prick the bubble then without causing major distress. An independent committee focused entirely on the valuation issue would be able to issue graduated warnings, from early in the episode. This would give both the authorities and investors more time to react.

In Britain the FSA has publicly taken the view that it is not its job to forecast the direction of house price movements. Nevertheless, in practice it has hinted strongly that it is worried and it has tried to warn banks of the dangers of overlending. An AVC would clearly provide support to this approach.

Some readers will smile at the idea of a committee of experts issuing cautions on asset price valuations. It is easy to imagine that a committee warning of a stock market bubble from 1997 onward would have lost all credibility by 2000. Indeed, traders would probably have started to regard its warnings as a contrary indicator! But in recent years, with the market deflated, its reputation would surely have been rather higher. A committee warning about house prices also might have been ignored by many people, especially if house prices had continued to rise. However, the committee would perhaps be able at least to restrain the bubble by putting off some potential buyers and also perhaps deterring some people from taking excessive speculative positions. It probably would have a limited impact, however, unless it really had some teeth, and we will return to this in a moment.

Is it realistic to think that a committee could agree on when to issue warnings? Independent finance academics often disagree widely on valuations. For example, should the US stock market trade around its long-term average PE ratio of 15 times or is a significantly higher ratio now justified by the prospect of strong economic growth and low inflation? In the late 1990s there were plenty of financial gurus who found ways to justify high stock valuations. And in recent years many respected researchers have argued that there are good reasons for higher house prices.

In the last chapter I argued that there are fundamental underpinnings to valuations and that it is possible to indicate the risks that a market is entering a bubble. If we take the range for stocks I have suggested, a PE multiple of 10–20, how would it have worked in the 1990s stock bubble? An amber warning would have been issued when the US market multiple exceeded 20 times earnings, as it did in late 1996 at just about the time of Alan Greenspan's warning of "irrational exuberance." And the red warning would have come when the market multiple started to exceed 25 times in early 1998 (a previously unknown level for the market). The amber warning would have been at an S&P 500 index level of about 700, while the red warning would have come with the S&P 500 index at 1,100.

If these warnings had been heeded by investors and especially if they had been backed by other policy measures, they might have prevented the index soaring to peaks in 2000 of over 1,500, before falling back to 800 in 2002. The extremes of the bubble and bust could have been smoothed out. And private investors and pension fund trustees would have had clear health warnings. Even with the index back at 1,100 at the end of 2003, a switch to bonds on the amber warning would have brought a better return over the intervening eight years, while a switch to either cash or bonds in 1998 would have provided far superior returns.

Or consider the bubbles in house prices now. An amber warning today in the US might help prevent house prices rising to hugely expensive valuations in the next few years and avoid a full bubble developing. For the UK market an amber warning would have been required in early 2001 and a red warning in early 2002, though it would have been necessary to warn earlier about London prices.

A number of objections have been voiced to the Asset Valuation Committee proposal. As indicated above, many people question whether a committee could ever agree, and the answer to this problem would have to be majority voting. That then begs the question of who would be appointed and according to what procedure. But if members of the committee were chosen for their experience and were genuinely independent of banks and brokers as well as the government and central bank, I suspect they would be a fairly conservative bunch and would broadly agree on the ranges I have suggested. And remember that their job would not be to forecast markets, only to warn about gross market misalignments.

So far the focus has been on how to avoid bubbles. However, there is also the risk of the opposite problem, overly pessimistic markets. The AVC could play an important role here too, if it could convince investors that markets were actually unduly cheap for the long term. At the very least, it could help make buying equities by long-term investors, such as pension funds and insurance companies, more respectable, and in a housing slump could encourage homebuyers or property investors to step up and buy. It would also have provided sound justification for the authorities' decision in 2002–3 to suspend insurance company solvency requirements, which were threatening the market by forcing insurance companies to sell more stocks.

Investors do tend to exhibit herd-like behavior. So the idea of an Asset Valuation Committee can be seen as providing the herd with a group of "wise elders" to moderate the wild stampedes first in one direction and then in another. But it could also be helpful in advising government agencies when they should be thinking of other possible measures to control bubbles. And this could be the way to give it real teeth, as we shall see below.

170

NONMONETARY MEASURES TO CONTROL BUBBLES

With monetary policy an uncertain instrument for managing bubbles, governments need alternatives. There is a range of tax and regulatory approaches that might help, known in the jargon as micro policies.[8] One area to explore is whether taxes could be used to discourage buyers and therefore help to prevent bubbles developing. For example, tax deductibility on mortgages could be scaled back when prices are high. In the UK mortgage interest relief was phased out fully in 2000–1 but in other countries, including the US, Netherlands, and Ireland, tax deductibility of mortgage interest is still allowed to a substantial degree. Tax deductibility is not necessarily a prime cause of property bubbles. After all, it does not exist now in the UK and its value has been reduced in other countries by lower marginal tax rates and lower interest rates. But it does help provide the fuel when bubble expectations develop.

Another approach would be to raise property taxes or transaction taxes. For example, an additional annual property tax levy of 0.5 percent of the value of a property should cut property prices by a multiple, because the extra tax would have to be paid every year. Raising transaction taxes such as stamp duties might help too.

The tax attractions of investment property could also be reduced. In Australia, depreciation was reduced early in 2004 and there has also been a lively debate over whether the practice of "negative gearing" should be discontinued. Negative gearing, which is not permitted in most countries, allows Australian investors with costs exceeding rental income to offset the loss against their income taxes. However, supporters of negative gearing argue that it encourages the provision of rental property and helps to keep rents down. Other governments are keen to promote the private rental market, so may be reluctant to disturb the tax arrangements for rental property.

Moreover, raising taxes to restrain a property bubble is not going to be easy politically. Higher taxes are never popular and if they are aimed at restraining house price growth they could be doubly unpopular. Perhaps if they were explicitly linked to offsetting cuts in income taxes there might be greater acceptance, but there are always winners and losers in big tax shifts and the losers tend to complain loudly.

The other problem is that if people believe house prices are going to continue to rise rapidly, higher property taxes may not deter them from buying anyway. Certainly that has been the British experience in recent years, where both property taxes and stamp duties have been pushed up considerably but have not stopped house prices rising. Of course, in the other direction, if the bubbles go bust and prices go below sensible valuations a cut in these taxes would be popular. The trouble is that a significant fall in house prices would make the economy weak and put government budgets under pressure, so cutting property taxes might be difficult.

Some people have suggested that making owner-occupied houses subject to capital gains tax could limit housing bubbles. In the UK they are exempt and in the US gains of up to $500,000 for a couple are excluded. No government keen to encourage labor mobility would want to put a tax on gains if people are simply moving house, so capital gains would presumably only be payable if people were trading down to a cheaper place. But then the result would be that people would be less likely to trade down. A tax on capital gains could therefore make the bubble worse.

RESTRAINING BANK LENDING

A much more fruitful approach, particularly for property bubbles, is to find some way to put speed limits on bank lending during booms. Two ideas doing the rounds of financial regulation conferences at the moment are countercyclical capital standards and stabilizing provisioning rules. The first would require banks to have higher capital ratios when the economy is booming and allow lower ratios when the economy is weak.[9] Capital ratios could also be varied according to whether or not bubbles seem to be emerging in stocks and property (perhaps based on AVC assessments, as discussed above). In practice, banks tend to have pro-cyclical capital ratios; that is, lower capital ratios during booms and bubbles and higher ones during recessions and busts. And even if their official capital ratios are not pro-cyclical, risk assessment often becomes more relaxed during booms while off-balance-sheet activity such as guarantees and derivatives may be stepped up, which comes to the same thing.

Stabilizing provisioning rules would operate in a countercyclical way too, requiring banks to make larger provisions against losses when times are good and smaller ones when the economy is weak.[10] Such a system was introduced in Spain in 2000 and has been avidly studied by regulators.[11] However, this would require flexibility from accounting standards setters. Moreover, in most countries the tax authorities are reluctant to make such provisions tax deductible, because of fears that banks would use them as a tax avoidance measure. Spain has a complex system, but it does allow banks to influence how much extra provisioning they make in the good times. An approach that might satisfy the tax authorities would be for the supervisors to determine the extra provisioning, based on the mix of lending and the behavior of asset prices. For example, if house prices are seen as high, banks could be required to hold larger reserves against new mortgages, while if the stock market is high margin lending could be limited.

A more direct approach to restraining bank lending during house price bubbles is to impose limits on loan-to-value ratios (LTVs). Hong Kong actively used this technique in the 1990s. As early as 1991 the Hong Kong Monetary Authority (HKMA) reduced its guideline LTV limit from 90 percent to 70 percent. In fact, banks were generally more cautious than this and as of September 1997, approximately the peak of the boom, actual LTVs were only at 52 percent.[12] The HKMA also issued a guideline in 1994 that banks should limit their property exposure to 40 percent of loans. These measures helped to largely protect the banking system despite the subsequent 65 percent fall in house prices. Individuals lost much of their equity in housing, but the default rate on loans was relatively low.

However, this policy did not prevent a major bubble because there were enough new lenders entering the market to ensure that mortgages were easily available and buyers were often so keen to purchase that they took out personal loans at high interest rates to cover the downpayment. Perhaps without the LTV limit the bubble would have inflated even further, but the Hong Kong experience strongly suggests that an LTV limit, on its own, is not enough.

Another approach to limiting house price bubbles would be to release more land for development if prices start rising rapidly. In some parts of the world, for example in the Mid West of the US, land is readily available and house builders respond quickly to changes in demand and prices. But in many places, governments control land use and they may not be very responsive to market conditions.

Kate Barker, in her official *Review of Housing Supply*, identified this as one of the problems in Britain in 2004.[13] She therefore proposed a number of changes that would require officials to take account of changes in house prices in their local area when they release land for housing. In principle, if the authorities automatically released new land for building as soon as prices started to rise, bubbles could be restrained. Even though properties would take time to build, speculation would be deterred.

The best way would be to give local authorities a strong incentive to release land, for example by enabling them to auction planning permissions. But the incentives and institutional arrangements need to be clear. The Hong Kong government has exactly these powers, but failed to use them in the early and mid-1990s, partly because of lobbying by the large developers but also because it was afraid of causing a housing crash.

Measures to restrain stock market bubbles are more difficult. Taxes on transactions are not desirable, because it is important to maintain liquidity in markets. One policy sometimes suggested for limiting the downside is to ban or restrict short selling. When markets are falling, they sometimes take on the look of a bubble in reverse. People pile in and sell stocks, not just securities they own but also some they don't. They are hoping that, having sold the stock for delivery at a date in the future, the market price will have fallen by then and they can buy the stock to "deliver" it to the buyer at a lower price.

In practice, it is difficult to eliminate short selling. As usual in the markets, if governments cut off one way of doing something, ingenious people find another way. However, the main objection to banning short selling is that it might, paradoxically, have the effect of making bubbles more likely. Banning short selling makes it more difficult for speculators to bet against an uptrend. Arguably therefore, short selling should be made easier and more fashionable precisely as a way of limiting the upside.

Fortunately, recent developments in the financial markets are in the right direction. As we saw in Chapter 1, for retail investors new products such as CFDs (contracts for difference), ETFs (exchange trade funds), and spread betting make it easier to go short. And for institutional investors (and to an increasing extent private investors too), the growing importance of hedge funds means that short selling is now much more common among pension funds and insurance companies.

A more radical measure that could be applied both to stocks and housing is to require health warnings on market levels from brokers or real estate agents, once the Asset Valuation Committee has issued a bubble warning. Such a warning could be required to be included on statements or on promotional literature, rather like on cigarette packets. "Buying now could seriously damage your wealth" comes to mind.

Warnings might have some impact, though the problem always is going to be that, if prices continue to rise, people will question the committee's view. It also has the practical difficulty that some stocks, either individually or by industry, and some housing regions might not be sharing in a particular bubble. The committee might need to be fairly specific, which could become tricky in practice. Another difficulty for the committee is that it would need to start warning early in a price rally. If it waited until prices have already surged to obviously high levels, it may itself prick the bubble.

What about if asset prices are weak? Are there any specific measures that governments can take? An extreme approach is that of some Asian countries, including Japan, Hong Kong, and Taiwan, where governments have bought stocks directly to try to stop them falling further. The main danger arises if buying is done too early in a postbubble phase, when stocks have fallen but are not particularly cheap. The effect may then be to transfer the losses to the taxpayer, rather than to stabilize the market. Government purchases of stocks probably should only be contemplated in extreme bear markets or if confidence is particularly low. Again, the AVC could be the arbiter here, in indicating when the markets are really low.

Government purchases of property are less likely to be successful because, unless the property is kept empty, the overall supply to the market does not change once it is rented out. An alternative strategy could be to restrict the supply of land or of new planning permissions, as has been attempted in Hong Kong since 1999. But in some countries, such as the UK, the supply of new properties is very small relative to the existing stock anyway.

Taken together, all the micro measures described above could have some effect, especially if they were backed up by strong warnings from an Asset Valuation Committee. However, they would need to be implemented promptly and decisively since bubbles can emerge in a relatively short time frame, at least compared to the usual government speed of reaction.

One question worth asking is whether a government is likely to use these measures given the political pressures on it. When asset prices are rising, deliberate measures to restrain them will often be unpopular, so governments may indeed drag their feet. The time taken to implement many measures will often be too long anyway. By the time they are implemented the market may have run up far more and entered the dangerous stage.

The answer to this is an argument analogous to the case for independent central banks controlling monetary policy. An AVC would need to be equally independent and any policy actions based on its assessments would need to be automatic and not subject to government interference. Just as monetary policy committees directly control interest rates, an AVC might need to control capital and reserve requirements directly. Or, at the very least, the authorities that do control them should be required to consider the AVC's views directly.

If asset prices are falling there is much more political pressure for intervention, particularly if the decline affects a large number of people. The democratization of asset holdings discussed in this book suggests that there may indeed be increasing political pressure in the twenty-first century to put a floor under prices. A market collapse is less likely to result in popular glee that the speculators have lost out. But this brings us back to monetary policy, because central bankers are often very keen to help, either because of the disruptive effects of sudden falls in asset prices or because of the depressive effects on economic activity.

MONETARY POLICY IN AN ASSET BUST

So what should central banks do when asset prices fall and did Alan Greenspan get it right in 2001–3? The first point is that it is vital to avoid a systemic banking crisis, which could turn a bear market and a recession into a depression. This means that the central bank needs to stand ready at all times to provide a "lender of last resort" facility, lending freely to any bank in a liquidity crisis so that its problems do not result in a general panic.

The lesson was originally learnt by Britain as long ago as 1866 after the Overend Gurney crisis, generally agreed to be the last systemic financial crisis in the UK.[14] Early that year Overend Gurney, a large, long-established bank, faced difficulties with its loan portfolio when interest rates rose sharply from 3 to 8 percent. It asked for help from the Bank of England, but was refused. Over the next couple of days there were runs on banks all over London as depositors panicked and tried to withdraw their funds. Several banks failed, including a number of basically solvent ones. The authorities finally realized the dangers in the situation. The government suspended the Bank Charter Act, which forbade the issue of new bank notes, and the Bank of England gave assurances that it would freely provide support to the banking system. This broke the panic and nothing like it has been seen since in the UK.

In the 1930s the Federal Reserve failed to avoid systemic banking problems, partly because of the Gold Standard operation that made it difficult to cut interest rates, but also because it was too slow to react. This lesson was belatedly learnt and in recent history the Fed has several times needed to move quickly to reassure markets, notably in 1987 (after the stock market crash), 1998 (after the LTCM failure), and 2001 (after the September 11th terrorist attacks).

Deposit insurance is another way to limit the risk of a systemic banking crisis. However, in a major crisis such schemes usually are either not sufficiently comprehensive or lack the funds to calm everybody's nerves, so it may be necessary for governments to offer a blanket deposit guarantee, as in Japan from 1998. Even this will not work, however, if people doubt whether the government can afford it, as in Indonesia in 1997–8 and Argentina in 2001–2. On both occasions the government itself was plainly close to insolvency (plus there was distrust of government competence and integrity), so people wanted to withdraw funds and move their money overseas.

The second thing to do in an asset bust (in fact related to the first) is to maintain the money supply. Even those economists who question the overall monetarist approach nevertheless pay attention to this issue. The difficulty is that although the central bank can ensure that banks have lots of reserves available, banks may not wish to lend and borrowers may not wish to borrow, so broader measures of the money supply (which is what really matters) may not be so easily maintained. For most of the period from 1960 to 2001 central banks could reduce interest rates substantially and push them below the rate of inflation, which was enough to restimulate the economy. But with inflation low everywhere now, generating negative real interest rates will not be so easy in future.

We saw in Chapter 3 how Japan has struggled with this problem in recent years. Ultimately, central banks *can* maintain the money supply, but they may need to purchase an enormous quantity of assets to do so. Buying government bonds is the conventional approach, but they could also buy private-sector bonds, foreign bonds, or even stocks. The idea is to pump cash into the economy and lower yields as far along the yield curve as possible. Of course, this could start to look like an asset price support operation; which, in a sense, it is.

Finally, a degree of international policy coordination is desirable. Clearly, it is important to avoid protectionist measures, another major mistake in the 1930s. There are times also when coordinated interest rate cuts or expansionary fiscal policy may be useful to help restore confidence. In the 1930s one of the problems was competitive devaluation, where countries tried to devalue their way out of the recession. This worked relatively well for the UK, which departed from the Gold Standard early, but just put more pressure on the US. In recent years there have been signs of competitive devaluation again, with Japan and other

Asian countries buying huge amounts of dollars to prevent their currency rising. Again, this puts pressure on the US but, so far, the combination of the huge budget deficit and buoyant private spending has been able to sustain the US recovery and carry the whole world along.

The policies described above represent the current central bank orthodoxy on how to deal with an asset bust. I think that the orthodoxy is broadly correct and also that Greenspan has followed it very effectively—but perhaps too effectively. The key problem is how to calibrate the response. If the monetary stimulus is too vigorous, the asset bubble may simply be shifted to another asset, as we are seeing now in the case of housing. And in a worst-case scenario, particularly if there is a great deal of debt in the economy, the result of overstimulus can be inflation.

THE CHOICE: DEBT DESTRUCTION, BAILOUT, OR INFLATION

Ultimately financial crises, fiscal sustainability, and inflation are intertwined. When there is excessive private debt in an economy, a collapse in asset prices leaves the excess exposed and puts the banking system in jeopardy. There are only three ways out: debt destruction, bailout, or inflation. Debt destruction—where debts are reduced through a combination of bankruptcies and businesses and households paying off loans—is a very painful process, which nearly always makes the economy weak. Governments are determined to avoid this now and, provided that the government itself does not already have too much debt, it can simply bail out the private debtors, taking over their obligations and turning them into government debt, to be repaid out of taxes over time. This was the solution for the Thai government after the Asian crisis, because it had run surpluses for years before the crisis. But if government debt is already high the only alternative left is inflation, which lets debtors off the hook but means that creditors are repaid in devalued money.

If a very stimulatory monetary policy simply shifts the bubble to another area, the true bust may be postponed rather than averted. This shifts the burden back on the government again and back to the three options. The debt destruction option will always be the least palatable to governments, so we should expect to see bailouts as long as possible, both through low interest rates and fiscal measures if necessary. However, if the problems become sufficiently large a dose of inflation could be the final outcome. Mr. Greenspan has been successful in avoiding deflation so far, but it is too early to be sure that he has not laid the groundwork for a bout of inflation in coming years.

In conclusion, given the difficulties of dealing with the aftermath of a bubble, I suspect that in future there will be more pressure on the authorities to find ways to avoid, or at least limit, them in the first place. The most promising areas are capital and/or reserve requirements to limit bank lending. One positive trend is the move in many countries to coordinate the regulation of different parts of the financial sector, which has sometimes been done on a piecemeal basis in the past. Unfortunately this trend is less obvious in the US, where banks are still regulated by several different institutions: the Securities and Exchange Commission looks after brokerage and investments, while OFHEO oversees Freddie Mac and Fannie Mae.

There is another, very serious worry. The approach now is often to separate "macrofinancial stability" from regulation and supervision, with the former left as part of the central bank. This may make it more difficult to find an effective way to restrain bank lending during bubbles, unless the central bank and the supervisory authorities coordinate extraordinarily well.

Still, many people resist increased regulation or interference in markets on principle. Others resist this during a bubble because it interferes with them making money. Bubbles make a lot of money for early movers as well as agents, brokers, dealers, and often banks. Many also reject the AVC proposal, believing that valuation should be left to the market and, in any case, nobody would take such an institution seriously. But as well as playing an important role in advising the authorities, this committee could also be helpful to investors. With governments and central banks still not well prepared to prevent bubbles or to control their aftermath, investors can use all the help they can find.

12 STRATEGIES FOR INVESTORS

Perhaps in future governments will be able to use some of the measures discussed in the previous chapter to steer asset prices on a more stable course. But this is certainly not guaranteed and, on past experience, huge swings in asset prices will continue. Most central bankers take the orthodox view that it is a case of investor beware! So individuals need to think very carefully about their own asset position, what level and types of risks they are exposed to and whether they are on course to meet their financial objectives.

AFTER THE STOCK BUBBLE

People tend to view their assets exactly the wrong way round. After a bull run in stocks, they expect further strong increases and tend to believe that they are wealthier than they really are. If stocks are depressed they believe that they are poor, when in reality there is a good chance of a recovery.

Generally, for people at least five years from retirement a fall in the stock market is *good* news, because it offers the chance to buy stocks at a lower price. Of course, this is not true for older people trying to live off accumulated savings. For them a fall in the market is definitely not good news, which is why older people are usually best off holding a smaller proportion of stocks.

A rough rule of thumb is that the proportion of cash and bonds in someone's portfolio should be the same as their age. Someone aged 30 could therefore keep cash and bond holdings to 30 percent and have 70 percent in stocks, while aged 70 they should only have 30 percent in stocks. But this is only an approximate guide and a great deal also depends on what kind of stocks are in the portfolio as well as the individual's willingness to take risks.

Ideally, there would be something like an Asset Valuation Committee available to help people decide whether prices are high or not, as suggested in Chapter 11, but in its absence people will have to rely on commentators and their own judgment. In Chapter 10 I argued that the price–earnings ratio could be used as a rough indicator and that levels above 20 are normally a good warning signal. The only exception might be in the late stages of a recession or early in an upturn when profits are depressed and the PE ratio may be artificially high for a while, set to come down rapidly once earnings recover.

Exactly how to respond to high valuations depends partly on the individual's risk tolerance and also on how closely they are monitoring the market. Somebody who is watching the market daily and is willing to take a risk might be prepared to stay in stocks and try to ride the upswing. This style of investing, momentum investing, does nothing to iron out bubbles and busts but it can work for individuals, provided that they sell when the market starts to fall and are not tempted back in again too easily at slightly lower levels. Nevertheless, I doubt if many people buying into the market at the height of the 1999–2000 period were really thinking that they were riding a wild bubble. I suspect that most were simply caught up in the euphoria. If they saw small falls as buying opportunities rather than potentially the beginning of a major bear market, they probably lost money once the bear market really got going.

Someone who has only a passing interest in the markets and invests for the long term in a pension or in funds cannot afford to take the risk of trying to ride the bubble. For this type of investor, if they see that valuations are high or that a bubble is developing, the best strategy is normally to reduce weightings in stocks and increase in bonds and/or cash or property (depending on valuations). I would not suggest that this means selling out of stocks completely, except possibly for someone who cannot face any risk. It means reducing stockholdings and increasing other holdings. If the stock market rises higher after that it means reducing stockholdings further.

This is tough to do in practice during a bubble, because not only are most other people actively buying but they are also talking excitedly about the market. The reality is that a bubble is a very dangerous time for investors and yet most people perceive it as exactly the opposite. They believe that a major downward move is unlikely and that a new investment is highly likely to make money, often quickly.

In contrast, when the market falls substantially, people tend to believe that stocks are now hopeless, a losing investment. In fact an opportunity is arising, particularly if stocks go to low valuations. Of course, this will likely be when the economy is looking weak or political factors are scaring business and investors. But it is nevertheless an opportunity to buy at low levels, which normally comes right in the end. Again the momentum investor, trying to ride the bust, is at risk of being short the market just when it starts to turn up. Some day traders enjoyed happy times in 2001–2 by being continuously short the market, until it turned in 2003 and they were slow to switch to a bull strategy.

The approach I am recommending is sometimes known as contrarianism. It is based on the idea that markets swing back and forth and so, generally, the best strategy is to take the opposite view. However, markets do tend to exhibit a degree of momentum in the short term. In other words there is a tendency, albeit slight, for a market that rises today to rise some more tomorrow, at least for a while. So very nifty traders may be able to exploit that, provided that they don't get caught up in the mood too much, while contrarian investors may have to wait a while before they are on the right side of the move.

However, market timing is very, very difficult. That is why it is hard to recommend either the momentum-driven approach or the strict contrarian approach described above. And it is also why I am not suggesting that anybody should try either to sell out entirely or to load up indiscriminately on shares or any other asset class. The answer is to shift weightings somewhat, within certain limits. As an illustration, consider someone aged 50, aiming to have 50 percent of their portfolio in stocks on average. As the bubble inflated they would ideally have reduced their portfolio to 40 percent or perhaps 30 percent by early 2000, but probably not less.

Obviously they would have missed out on some of the upswing and would have lost some money in the downswing when even 30 percent was too much. But compare this to what most people did. As the market went higher, they became more and more enthusiastic about stocks and committed more and more funds. For example, the proportion of Americans owning mutual funds rose from 31 percent in 1994 to 48 percent in 2000.[1] Often they put most into the fastest-rising stocks, such as technology companies. Of course, this process is what drove the market higher. Many investment professionals including pension funds, to their shame and embarrassment now, did the same.

Similarly, in 2002–3 there was a great deal of fear in the market and many investors felt that it was not a good time to hold stocks. Ideally though, investors would have been starting to buy, increasing the share of stocks in their portfolios back toward the neutral 50 percent level. US stocks never became really cheap so it would have been hard, in 2002–3, to justify going heavily overweight. Some European and Asian markets did become unusually cheap, however.

Note, by the way, that if stocks are outperforming bonds and cash, as they were during the late 1990s, doing nothing will in itself increase the proportion of stocks in a portfolio just through a valuation effect. This is why some experts recommend keeping a fixed ratio of stocks, bonds, and cash and periodically "rebalancing" the portfolio. Rebalancing need only be done annually, or twice a year at most.[2]

One of the most successful investors of all time, Warren Buffett, takes a contrarian approach. He is often characterized as a long-term investor, which is correct, but he is not simply a buy-and-hold investor. He does reduce weightings if share prices go above what he sees as sensible levels and then he buys when everybody else is panicking and selling. During the late 1990s he several times commented on the bubble in the market and refused to buy technology stocks on the grounds that he did not understand them. For a while, as the bubble inflated further, his phenomenal popularity among investors waned, but when the market crashed he was suddenly back on top. And in early 2003 when US bond yields descended as low as 3.1 percent (10-year Treasuries), he sold a vast amount, just before prices dropped in a minicrash.

At the time of writing, stocks have recovered from the 2000–3 bear market and valuations are near the top of my range for the US, though still on more modest valuations for Europe. As I have discussed, some people worry that the bear market was not in fact severe enough to purge the market completely of speculation and excess. Normally after such a major bull run, indeed the largest for the US in the twentieth century, the final low would take us back to the bottom of my valuation range, a point where nearly everybody has utter revulsion for stocks.

That this has not happened is justifiable by the very strong policy response of the US authorities and the signs of a healthy economic recovery. But it is potentially dangerous for the future, because it could mean that the current rally gradually extends in the next couple of years to valuation levels that are again too high, as people are drawn back in. I do believe that there is room for modest gains from today's levels (i.e., the S&P 500 at 1,100), but if the index continues to rise strongly in 2005 and 2006 this will already be right at the limit of the reasonable range and investors should probably be cautious and begin to go underweight.

Valuations at the high end of the range are always vulnerable to severe bad news, such as political troubles or a recession. But also, after a period of particularly low interest rates in recent years, there is a question over how well the market will react as rates are normalized. Higher US interest rates are inevitable in 2005–6 unless the economy slows. So stocks will have to face either higher rates or a slow economy, either of which will present the market with headwinds.

SURVIVING THE PROPERTY BUBBLE

Property is the bubble that should be worrying individuals most at the moment. In Part II I argued that there are clear signs of an already inflated bubble in the UK, Australia, Spain, and the Netherlands—to name the most flagrant examples—and an emerging bubble in the US, particularly in certain areas.

Investors in property and homeowners need to heed the example of stocks. Returns on owning property have been stellar in recent years, with multiyear gains of 15–20 percent per annum or more in the UK, Australia, Spain, and several other countries and 5–10 percent per annum in many parts of the US. Prices for many homeowners have doubled in just a few years. But now valuations are very high, which means that the prospects are for much smaller gains or, very likely, losses in coming years. This is particularly so because general inflation is much lower than in previous house price cycles. Just as for stocks in the late 1990s, this is therefore a time for *reducing* exposure to this market. Moreover, unlike stocks, property usually cannot be sold at a moment's notice, so the strategy of trying to ride the bubble to the top is extremely dangerous.

Investors should consider selling some of their properties while homeowners should think about downsizing their position by trading down to a smaller property or a cheaper area. In practice, this option is probably going to make sense mainly for people planning to retire or have a major lifestyle change, such as moving to another country or opening a bed and breakfast. However, others who should perhaps consider it are those with very large debts relative to incomes.

It may also be possible to hedge property positions to a limited extent. For example, in the UK spread bets on housing are available, but the difficulty is that such bets can never exactly match the price performance of a particular property. Another approach is to consider buying government bonds and/or foreign assets, which would be likely to perform well if housing goes through a major correction because the economy would be very weak for a while and the currency would fall.

Of course, everyone needs a place to live so to sell up altogether is technically to go short the market relative to their natural position. And being short would be expensive if consumer price inflation were to go up sharply over the next few years, taking house prices with it. But, just as with the stocks bubble, perhaps what is most important is not to get carried away with rising prices and actually to buy at this point, trading up or buying a second home or an investment property.

Investors in property need to be particularly careful here, particularly if they have high levels of debt. In recent years some people have built up a "property empire" after beginning with just one rental property. When the value of the first property rose they immediately remortgaged it and used the cash as a downpayment on another one. With prices doubling in just a few years, it has been possible to build up a large portfolio and get rich quickly, at least on paper. However, if most of those properties are now held against large mortgages, only a comparatively modest fall in house prices could completely wipe out all the gains of recent years and take the investors back to square one or worse. Such an investor would be wise to sell at least some properties, both to take profits and to raise cash in case of need. Otherwise, in a worst-case scenario, they might need to sell a large number of properties under distressed conditions.

PENSIONS AND RETIREMENT

Pensions have had a bad press in recent years and some people have given up in disgust. They nevertheless remain attractive for their tax benefits, particularly for higher-rate taxpayers. For example, assuming a top marginal tax rate of 40 percent, pension contributions start with a 66 percent gain over investments out of posttax income. Of course, fees and costs erode this benefit, but investments made out of posttax income still have to do extremely well for many years to catch up.

Stripping the pension idea to its simplest form, individuals need to acquire an asset during their working life that will then pay an adequate income during retirement. When money is saved into a funded pension, it can earn a return from investments so that, with the help of the "power of compound interest," it will be worth much more several decades later. This phenomenon of compound interest is why investment advisers always urge people to start saving into pensions as early as possible.

For example, on the assumption of a 3 percent annual investment return (in real terms), $1,000 invested for someone retiring at 65 will be worth $3,260 if it is tucked away at the age of 25 and can enjoy 40 years to compound, but only $1,800 if it is invested at the age of 45. In 20 years the investment gains $800, while in 40 years it gains $2,260, proportionally much more.

To obtain an income of two-thirds of final salary (typically the aim of a good defined-benefit scheme), individuals need to put aside (or have the company do so) 15–20 percent of salary every year from the age of 25 until 65. The exact amount depends on investment performance and the precise nature of the pension promise (for example, whether it is inflation indexed). That is what it takes to pay out two-thirds of salary for the average 20 years or so life expectancy after 65. Again, we see the power of compound interest. Though the amount invested is only around 20 percent of salary for 40 years, individuals can expect to receive a pension for 20 years after that worth 67 percent of salary. But the size of the payments required into the fund is sensitive to investment returns, which is where the mistakes were made during the bubble years.

With many defined-benefit schemes now closed to new members (and in some cases to existing members), the investment risk has shifted back to employees. In principle, this might make little difference to the final pension paid, if companies paid in the same amount to defined-contribution schemes as they did to the old schemes. However, many have taken the opportunity to cut their average contribution and this does mean an inferior pension for employees eventually, unless they top up their contributions. In the UK there have already been strikes over this issue and it is likely to become an increasing bone of contention.

However, much also depends on investment performance and the markets. Poor results mean that the final pension will be disappointing or people may have to remain at work longer than they had hoped. Also if the markets fall sharply just before retirement employees may lose out, though, properly managed, this should not be a problem because when approaching retirement the asset allocation should be switched gradually out of stocks and into fixed-income assets.

With a defined-benefit scheme individuals face a different risk—the risk that their company does not pay out the promised pension because it goes bankrupt. How certain can anybody be that even the most solid and respected of companies will still be around in 50 years' time?

As discussed in Chapter 4, companies are struggling to determine the best investment strategy for a defined-benefit scheme and the pendulum has swung toward holding relatively more bonds and less stocks. But for someone controlling their own pension fund, this might not be the right answer. Much depends on age. For a young or youngish individual, a large proportion of equities may be the best bet. Equities tend to outperform other assets over the long term. If they prove disappointing for a while there is plenty of time for them to recover and continuing contributions will go in at a cheaper price. Individuals, unlike companies, do not need to worry about the problems of mark-to-market accounting.[3] So provided that retirement is still at least 15 years off, the benchmark allocation should be to place a large proportion in equities. Of course, as noted above, when equities are expensive and especially when they appear to be in a bubble, the actual allocation should normally be under the benchmark.

What about someone in their late 50s or 60s coming up to retirement soon? Generally the advice should be that their pension scheme should hold more fixed-income assets. But remember that, though payments into the scheme may be ending in a few years, payments out are set to continue for around 30 years, still a long time in investment terms. So then it depends on the arrangements. If the whole pension will be used to buy an annuity at the moment of retirement, in just a few years, then the scheme should definitely be moving toward more bonds and less equities. And in the last few years just before the annuity is bought, it would be wise to be down to 20 percent or less in equities just in case the stock market dips. But if the pension fund will stay invested for longer, perhaps until the age of 75—the current latest date to buy an annuity in the UK—there is plenty of time for the fund to grow and it should continue to hold a large proportion of equities.

Does it make sense to include property in a pension fund? At the time of writing the British government is proposing changes to allow pension assets that would permit holding individual properties with the fund. And the property bubble is making some investors in the UK excited at the prospect. However, there are two reasons for caution. One is that if the bubble bursts, this could prove to be a very poor investment. More fundamentally, people need to be careful not to be overexposed to property.

For most people their own home is a vital long-term asset in that it provides them with a permanent place to live. Economists would say that owning a house represents a lifetime hedge against rents, which comes to much the same thing. Property is also a very useful hedge against inflation, which probably also says the same thing, and hedging against inflation is particularly important for pensioners who no longer enjoy a salary. But overreliance on investment properties could be a mistake. There is a high risk of a major fall in property prices that would take a decade or more to reverse.

BE REALISTIC ABOUT LIKELY RETURNS

During the 1990s many investors in stocks began to see double-digit returns as normal and expected them to continue indefinitely. In fact, not only were such high returns not likely to continue, but they made it likely that future returns would be *lower* than average. In Chapter 10 I set out the level of return above inflation that might be expected in different asset classes over the very long term, ranging from 2–4 percent in government bonds to 5–7 percent in stocks. I placed property in between, with real returns likely to be 4–6 percent per annum. But these are average gains over the long term. During a bubble they are wildly exceeded for several years and investors start to believe that the party can go on for ever. And then comes the bust and returns are way below these average levels, often negative, and again people start to see this as the norm and after a time give up.

Both of these attitudes are wrong. The sad fact is that over the long term, it is hard to turn a small amount of money into a large amount purely by buying assets. It can be done, but only by taking huge risks with large borrowings and by timing the markets exactly right. Somebody who avoids excessive debt and follows the under- and over-weighting strategies described above can certainly grow their wealth, but it is not a route from rags to riches. Generally, investing in assets is best seen as a way to preserve and modestly grow existing wealth. And the only reliable way to accumulate wealth in the first place is through work, whether salaried or entrepreneurial. In this sense people's greatest assets are their own abilities.[4]

It is vital to consider the risks of different investments. The risks are highest when valuations are high and lowest when they are low. However, as I hope I have made clear, deciding exactly when valuations are high and when they are low is not rocket science and there is plenty of room for being wrong, especially over short time horizons. Even after a major market fall that makes prices look cheap, there could be a further move down, either because the mood of investors is still negative or because of some more bad news.

Some active investors believe that the way to deal with market declines is to wait for clear technical indicators such as long-term moving averages to turn round before buying in again. But unless the period calculated for the moving average is short (which increases the risk that it is not a final bottom), the investor will miss the first part of the rise. And typically, if the technical analyst waits for strong confirmation of the turn, the market will already be up very substantially.

For most investors I think the risks just have to be accepted. Stocks can fall and they can fall substantially, with the downside for a portfolio of stocks easily in the 40–50 percent range as we have recently seen, and potentially more in a meltdown scenario. Property can fall too, with declines of 30–40 percent possible in a low-inflation environment and greater declines certainly possible also in a meltdown scenario.

Nevertheless, major bear markets offer an opportunity for the long-term investor to buy assets cheaply. Of course, it is often just as tough to buy when markets are collapsing as it is to sell (or sometimes just not to buy) when markets are bubbling. But when everybody is pessimistic about markets, a realistic view of likely long-term asset returns can give good results. Buying too early can feel painful. When markets fall further after a purchase, investors will wish they had waited longer. However, in the long run, if they buy when valuations are moderate they will do well.

My expectation is that residential property prices will fall in coming years, offering a new buying opportunity. Of course, if home prices go through a miserable period, many people will want to give up on property. But provided that rental yields rise significantly and house price–earnings ratios return to lower levels, property could again represent an attractive investment. However, it will be important to be patient. Major property price slumps typically take three to five years or more to work through. It would be dangerous to be seduced into buying by a small setback in the market, unless valuations are attractive too.

ASSET RETURNS DEPEND CRUCIALLY ON INFLATION

All the major asset classes do particularly well in certain economic environments and particularly badly in others. I am not thinking here in terms of months but years or even decades. And one of the most important variables is the rate of consumer price inflation. For example, in 2003 bonds were widely touted as the best asset class for the long term. Retail investors crowded into corporate bond funds, particularly in the first half of the year when stocks still seemed very risky. Pension funds and other institutional investors began to focus on bonds as the safest asset class to meet their future liabilities. But in fact conventional bonds are a highly risky investment if inflation should return. In the 1970s investors in bonds faced devastating losses, measured in real terms. Wealth held in bonds was eroded by 50–60 percent or more over certain periods of high inflation.

Of course, inflation may not return on that scale. In fact, I would be surprised if it did, at least for some years. Nevertheless, it could. If the current determination among central banks to avoid deflation at all costs leads to a surging economy, higher inflation could quickly take hold. Or if a new major war emerges from somewhere, inflation could be the most likely outcome. So nobody should think that conventional bonds are not a risky investment, especially in a longer-term perspective. A bond portfolio needs to be balanced by other assets that are protected against inflation. Still, on the basis of ongoing 2 percent per annum inflation, I have suggested that bond yields should be in the 4–6 percent range, so bonds will become an attractive buy if yields move up to near 6 percent in coming years.

A deflation scenario would hit property investments the worst. It could also be difficult for stocks, particularly those of higher-risk companies. So there is risk in every direction. The only truly safe investment is inflation-indexed government bonds, but these currently offer a yield of only about 2 percent above inflation. If inflation-indexed yields return closer to 3 percent they will be attractive again. However, to earn more than 2–3 percent above inflation, risk must be taken. The best answer in my view (and this is the conclusion of finance theory and the majority of investment professionals) is to hold a diversified portfolio including stocks, bonds, and property. Such a portfolio does not need to be actively traded.

The other area of risk that needs to be kept in mind is borrowing. When people believe that asset prices are going to rise rapidly they have little hesitation in taking on high levels of debt, relative to their income or, in the case of investment property, to rental streams. And yet periods where asset values will go up rapidly are likely to be limited, and after a bubble there is usually a bust. On average over time, mortgage rates are likely to be around 4–5 percent above inflation (official interest rates at about 2–3 percent above inflation with a mortgage spread of around 2 percent), so gains from borrowing to buy assets are usually going to be moderate rather than substantial. And if the assets are purchased when they are expensive, or if the borrower is hit by a bout of high interest rates, there is a real risk of distress.

TRY A STRESS TEST

One technique widely used by financial institutions is to "stress test" their financial position. This means asking what would happen in a worst-case scenario. In practice, banks normally do not take the very worst scenario they can imagine, because usually almost any portfolio is in deep trouble then. For example, how many households would be in difficulty if interest rates rose by 5 percent, property prices fell 65 percent, and stock prices fell 50 percent? That was the scenario that befell Hong Kong between 1997 and 2000 and it is a wonder that its economy did not do a lot worse!

A "reasonable" stress test for readers in the US, UK, and Australia might be to consider the impact of a 3 percent rise in interest rates, a 30 percent fall in home prices, and a (new) 40 percent decline in stocks. Such a scenario would obviously play havoc with many people's asset position. But the idea of the stress test is not to see whether you like it, but whether you would survive it! Would you be forced to sell the car? Or perhaps even your house? Would you be forced to default on debt? Would your retirement have to be drastically delayed? If the answer to any of these questions is yes, you may have too much risk. For younger people higher risk may be more acceptable because there would still be time to recover from losses by earning more money in future. For older people, there would be less scope.

One of the key themes of this book is to emphasize how important assets have become in our lives and yet how much risk and uncertainty attach to them. To find a safe way through the investment maze is not easy. Everybody needs to have a clear idea of all their assets and liabilities and the risks surrounding them in order to take good decisions, not just on where to invest but when to move jobs, whether to take on a new mortgage, and when to retire. What is important from the perspective of this book is not to get carried away by the increase in wealth (on paper) when stock or property prices rise and, equally, not to get too depressed when prices are low. The more that people handle assets sensibly and take decisions well, shying away from asset price booms and keeping their debt under control, the more likely it is that the overall market and the economy itself will be stable.

If there are just three things to remember about investing, they are these. First, regular savings coupled with the power of compounding add up to serious money given sufficient time—but you need to start early. Secondly, diversification helps to spread the risk and smooth the growth of assets. Thirdly, for anyone who is still earning money, falling asset prices should be regarded as an opportunity not a disaster, while rising asset prices should be regarded with caution rather than glee. And bubbles, when everybody sees the asset concerned as a wonderful investment, are especially dangerous. Once asset prices are seen in those terms, the opposite to the way most people view them, not only are investment decisions simpler, but it is also easier to sleep at night.

FINAL THOUGHTS: LIVING WITH BUBBLES

Exactly how Chairman Greenspan's super-stimulus policy will play out in the coming years is impossible to forecast. Some people are convinced that it will fail and that we are near the end of the bubble era. They anticipate a collapse of the housing bubbles before long and a new bear market in stocks, taking us below the levels seen in 2002. This, they believe, will finally extinguish investor exuberance for both assets and take us back to calmer, more realistic attitudes to investment. Meanwhile, debt will come to be viewed as a burden rather than an opportunity and people will shy away from borrowing, as they did in earlier times.

However, a simultaneous collapse in stocks and housing is inconceivable without a severe recession, or even worse. The pessimists tend to view this as a necessary purgative, to cleanse the system of the excesses of the Greenspan years and ready the economy for a new, healthier future, with a leaner financial sector and a greater focus on genuine economic development.

Nevertheless, it would not be a short, sharp shock. We have to imagine a period, lasting two to three years at least, with unemployment rising rapidly, companies going bankrupt in droves, pension schemes abandoned, numerous people losing their homes, and banks in serious trouble. Government finances would be in a monumental mess as deficits, already large, expanded with the downturn, while companies, pension schemes, banks, and householders clamored for bailouts.

The 1973–4 recession was the worst in postwar history for most countries—though the double dip during 1980–82 came close—but this scenario would be at least as bad and potentially much worse. There is a risk of a vicious downward spiral akin to the US in the 1930s or Japan in the 1990s, not least because we would almost certainly see a period of falling prices. Deflation would not be the end of the world of course, but the political consequences are impossible to foresee and the human impact for those affected would be severe.

This nightmare scenario cannot entirely be ruled out. Nevertheless, I believe that it would take a combination of policy mistakes that we should be able to avoid and external shocks that we should be able to mitigate. Moreover, I suspect that policy makers and the populace would rather risk renewed inflation than a deflationary slump.

Ultimately, bubbles arise because market behavior is not always rational and because governments and central banks are always more willing to support asset prices when they are falling than to lean against them when they are rising. And I am not sure that either is about to change. Indeed, globally more and more countries are liberating their banking systems and encouraging more lending to consumers. In recent years this has already caused upsets in some countries, including Taiwan and South Korea.

Perhaps the combination of mild busts in markets combined with improved investor education could help us avoid severe crashes. And perhaps some of the nonmonetary policy measures suggested in this book, such as warnings on valuations and active restraints on bank lending, could limit the worst excesses. However, I suspect that the price of preventing the disaster scenario is that bubbles will stay with us.

Governments and central banks will continue to try to prevent major economic slowdowns with easier monetary policy and expansionary fiscal policy. In the next downturn, unless interest rates have risen a great deal from 2004 levels, central banks will need to experiment with unconventional measures. But they are ready for that and, in theory at least, unconventional measures can work. With luck, Japan will be able to prove for sure that they do over the next few years as it finally recovers from the effects of the 1980s bubble.

The real test will come, however, if the desire to maintain economic growth and underpin asset prices conflicts with rising inflation. The last time that growth and inflation objectives collided in a big way

amid difficult circumstances was in the mid-1970s, when many countries chose to rekindle economic growth in the face of a major slump
but allowed inflation to become entrenched. It was the resulting
"stagflation" period of the late 1970s that convinced most people that
inflation had to be controlled. But if, in the next few years, we are faced
with a choice of either tolerating higher inflation or risking disastrous
asset declines, it will be interesting to see the choice that is made.

Central to this dilemma is that asset bubbles make the economy,
and potentially the whole financial system, unstable. When a bubble
deflates, whether deliberately pricked or because it collapses on its
own, the resulting economic slowdown is deflationary. But if central
banks let the bubble continue to inflate, sooner or later there is a risk
of inflation. And one scenario can flip over to the other alarmingly
quickly.

External shocks may play a key role. Shocks are unpredictable by
definition, though we can imagine the types of events that could
throw a spanner in the works. The Middle East has been the source of
most shocks in the last several decades, each of which has driven up
oil prices and in several cases caused recessions. But there are other
flashpoints around the world that could also lead to a sudden shift in
economic confidence, whether Taiwan or North Korea or even a major
terrorist attack.

Another possible shock is an economic or political crisis in China,
perhaps made more likely by the economic boom of recent years.
Spurred by low interest rates and a highly competitive currency (artificially held down by the government), China is going through a massive
investment boom. The stock market has been volatile but there are
signs of a property bubble emerging, particularly in office buildings and
luxury condominiums in Shanghai. China's economy has now become
large enough to play a major role in world economic growth, but the
volatility of its system, part private and part state controlled, creates particular risks. China often seems to have only two speeds, dead slow and
full speed ahead.

There are other types of shocks arising from bubbles and busts. The
bankruptcy of a major financial institution is one example. The seizure
of a market settlement system and a serious upset in the burgeoning

derivatives markets are others. Experience shows that the trigger for the collapse of a bubble does not have to be a major event and can sometimes be very small.

However, the effect of shocks would be to weaken the US and other major economies and, with luck, this can be offset with easier monetary and/or fiscal policy. So we come back to policy mistakes as the main risk for the future. And yet there is a nagging problem here. If policy continually aborts economic downturns and eases policy in response to asset price slumps, the imbalances grow ever larger and problems are simply stored up for the future.

There is a crucial need for governments to get a grip on fiscal deficits. If fiscal policy is gradually tightened in the next few years, interest rates will need to rise less rapidly and this will ease the pressure on markets. It is also vital that the gradual progress toward freer trade and the globalization of markets continues. This opens up new growth opportunities as well as helping to keep the lid on inflation. But ultimately, much will continue to depend on the central banks.

There is a view that inflation has retreated for ever, under the weight of globalization trends, fast productivity growth, and liberalized labor and product markets. However, this may be too sanguine and there is a risk that, before long, inflation will reemerge as a major worry. Suddenly the Fed might find itself with the need to raise interest rates much more sharply to slow the economy. Then the problem will be how to do this without crushing the housing market (and perhaps also the stock market if it continues to move up toward its 2000 highs). In 1999–2000 short- and long-term rates went to 6.5 percent before the economy slowed.

The UK is probably even more susceptible to an inflation scare because there is little spare capacity in the economy and very low unemployment. Strong economic growth could very quickly alarm the Bank of England, especially given the rapid growth of government spending. Past form suggests that interest rates of 6 percent or more would be needed to slow the economy. However, with household debt much higher than in the past and house prices so inflated, such a high level might not prove necessary, because even a moderate rise could bring a sharp pullback in consumer spending.

Elsewhere, the Reserve Bank of Australia faces similar difficulties to the Bank of England. But in early 2004 with the Australian property bubble showing signs of peaking, further tightening could be held back in 2005–6. Spain, Ireland, and the Netherlands, the other main countries with property bubbles, are at the mercy of the European Central Bank. Fortunately, with the German economy structurally weak, interest rates look like staying low for a while.

AN UNCERTAIN FUTURE

What will be the outcome? As forecasters know only too well, it is hard to make predictions, especially about the future! My best guess is that the world economic upswing that began in 2002 and accelerated in 2003–4 will continue and that the challenge in the near term will be managing a return to normal interest rates. Then, after a time, the problem will shift to the need to slow the economy amid renewed concern about inflation. Nevertheless, there are other possibilities.

One scenario is that the current upswing simply runs out of steam, even without inflation and central bank tightening. Recent strong growth may be due to temporary stimulus effects and there is a danger that the depressive effects of the stock market bust have not yet fully worked through. In particular, pension shortfalls both in corporate plans and in individuals' own investments could lead businesses and consumers to be cautious in their spending. Some people believe that the recovery in stocks in 2003 could prove to be a bear market rally and that the markets have yet to find their true low point, which they expect to be well below the lows seen in 2002–3 (about 780 on the S&P 500 index and 3,300 on the FTSE 100 index).

I share the pessimists' concern that many stock markets, particularly the US market, did not fall to especially low valuations in 2002–3, as typically happens at the true end of a bear market. However, if the economic upswing continues, profits will continue to recover and that should prevent stock markets revisiting their old lows, even if they do fall back from end 2003 levels. And there is still scope for further gains as long as the news is good. But there is no doubt that if the economic upswings falter, stock markets remain vulnerable. And as interest rates rise, stock market valuations will be under pressure, particularly in the US.

The behavior of bubbles is very hard to predict. They often continue to inflate far longer than seems possible. Again, my hunch about the emerging US housing bubble is that it will surprise everybody by continuing to grow in coming years. This is particularly likely if the Fed is slow to bring rates up to neutral levels, perhaps because economic growth slows a little or goes through a soft patch. But if confidence in stocks and housing fell, both markets could head south, dragging the economy down. Then the Fed and the government would be scrabbling for new economic stimulus measures. Unfortunately, an early and sharp economic slowdown, before the Fed has raised interest rates much and the government has got a grip on the budget deficit, would find the authorities with limited ammunition. Kick-starting the economy might prove harder than in 2001–3, when the authorities started with high interest rates and a budget surplus.

The housing bubbles in other countries are particularly vulnerable if the US economy takes an early tumble. As we have seen so often before, when the US economy sneezes others catch cold. Both Britain and Australia avoided a major economic slowdown in 2001 when the US suffered recession, though this was primarily due to the surge in house prices following cuts in local interest rates. House valuations are much higher now, far beyond historical peak levels, and it is difficult to see prices surging again, even with new cuts in rates.

Britain and Australia could also see a local collapse in their housing bubbles, independently of US events, the result of higher interest rates or a shock to confidence of some sort. Or if their economies remain strong, the collapse could be delayed until 2006–7 as inflation begins to return as a problem and monetary policy makers have no choice but to raise rates above neutral levels to slow the economy.

House price bubbles are inextricably linked with rising consumer debt. Debt in itself does not create a problem if it is solidly backed, but if it is backed only by overvalued assets it creates a serious vulnerability. The rapid increases in household debt seen in the US, UK, Australia, and many other countries will prove a major burden if house prices fall. And if this is combined with rising unemployment and a general recession, the problems could become even greater.

Nevertheless, if we are lucky, all the adjustments that are necessary in the economy can be handled gradually over time. Lower house prices and higher savings rates could be offset by stronger investment, high productivity growth, and steady incomes growth. In the US a reduced budget deficit and higher household savings could balance out a fall in the current account deficit. Continuing economic recovery could give time for these adjustments so that, come the next economic downturn for whatever reason, neither house prices nor consumer debt look too exposed. And if budget deficits can be returned to surplus during the upturn while central banks nudge up interest rates, there would be replenished fiscal and monetary ammunition to deal with the next economic downturn.

Central banks face a tough job navigating around the worst-risk scenarios, but two recent trends in the economy could help them enormously, if they continue. One is low inflation. As long as inflation stays low central banks are not under pressure to hike interest rates to try to slow the economy. Most economists of my generation are instinctively fearful of renewed inflation and see it around every corner. But inflation was slow to pick up during the last economic upswing and perhaps it will remain sluggish for longer than suggested by the old models. Global competition and highly liberalized labor markets both point that way, though only time will tell.

The second positive factor is productivity growth. The US has been enjoying an extraordinary period of productivity growth in recent years, linked to cost cutting and better use of computer and networking technology. If this fast growth can be maintained, not only will it contribute to keeping inflation low but also it will allow incomes to grow relatively fast, helping the economy to manage high levels of debt. Somewhat puzzlingly, fast productivity growth has yet to take hold in Europe, though perhaps it will pick up in coming years as new investment increasingly incorporates the new technology.

However, strong growth and low inflation are also a recipe for expanding asset bubbles if we are not careful. We need to find new ways to keep asset prices and debt within reasonable ranges to take some of the pressure off monetary policy. But I am not optimistic that new measures will be introduced soon. So the monetary policy makers will have to deal with the housing bubbles without help. If they fail, the risk scenarios loom large. For all our sakes I hope it is not too exciting a ride!

NOTES

INTRODUCTION

1 Probably the two best books on the history of bubbles are Charles Kindleberger, *Manias, Panics and Crashes*, Basic Books, 1978 and Edward Chancellor, *Devil Take the Hindmost*, Plume, 2000.
2 Kindleberger, *op cit.*

CHAPTER 1

1 See the discussion of Minsky's model in Kindleberger, *op cit*, pp 15–24. The original can be found in Hyman P. Minsky, "Financial stability revisited: The economics of disaster," in *Board of Governors of the Federal Reserve System, Reappraisal of the Federal Reserve Discount Mechanism*, Washington DC, June 1972, vol. 3, pp 95–136. Minsky's model is an elucidation of a pattern also set out by economists such as John Stuart Mill and Alfred Marshall in the nineteenth century and Knut Wicksell and Irving Fisher in the early twentieth century.
2 Much of the data in this book is sourced from Thomson Datastream. Another good source for US market data is www.spglobal.com/earnings.
3 "Buy to let" was coined by the UK Association of Retail Letting Agents in the mid-1990s to help encourage more individuals to invest in property for letting.
4 Some people talk of bond market bubbles and currency bubbles. I do not believe it is useful to talk of bond market bubbles for the following reason. Bond yields can indeed go to low levels at times (as for example in mid-2003 when US Treasury yields touched 3.1 percent). But this reflected the view that inflation might disappear altogether and give way to deflation. Perhaps this view was unrealistic, and indeed bond yields quickly reversed when new signs of strength

appeared in the US economy, but it was certainly a plausible view. I prefer to reserve the term bubble for markets where prices become exceptionally high in *real* terms, in relation to earnings in the case of stocks or wages and rents in the case of housing.

Currencies can also become overvalued relative to underlying trade performance, and sometimes these overvaluations last a long time, if financing is available. Commonly, countries with a bubble in stocks or in housing have high currency valuations too, as for example in the US in the late 1990s when the US dollar reached $0.82 vs the euro; or more recently in the case of sterling, which has long been uncomfortably high against the euro and in 2004 surged to $1.90 vs the dollar. These overvaluations often reflect the inflow of money into the country, linked to the bubble in stocks or housing. But it is rare to see a pure currency bubble, on its own.

5 See for example Ivo Arnold, Peter van Els, and Jakob de Haan, *Wealth Effects and Monetary Policy*, Research Memorandum WO No 719, December 2002, De Nederlandsche Bank. Also Karl E. Case, John M. Quigley, and Robert J. Shiller, *Comparing Wealth Effects: The Stock Market Versus the Housing Market*, Cowles Foundation Discussion Paper No. 1335, October 2001.

6 For a recent survey see Jose Martins Barata and Luis Miguel Pacheco, *Asset Prices and Monetary Policy: Wealth Effects on Consumption*, Centro de Investigacao sobre Economia Financeira, Lisbon, February 2003. Also, OECD *Economic Outlook 75*, June 2004, p 134.

7 401K accounts are a defined-contribution pension fund that is under the control of the employee and can be actively switched between stocks, mutual funds, bonds, and cash.

8 Arnold, van Els, and de Haan, *op cit*.

CHAPTER 2

1 I have drawn on a variety of sources for the discussion of the 1920s and 1930s. Chancellor, *op cit*, is particularly well written and colorful. Another very readable and worthwhile source is "The ups and downs of capitalism: Ben Bernanke on the 'Great Depression' and

the 'Great Inflation,'" an interview with introduction by Brian Snowdon, *World Economics*, Vol. 3, No. 2, April–June 2002, pp 125–70. A detailed, statistical approach is found in Christopher Dow, *Major Recessions: Britain and the World 1920–1995*, Oxford University Press, 1998. Another general resource is Peter Temin, *Did Monetary Forces Cause the Great Depression?*, Norton, 1976.

2 Jim Potter, *The American Economy Between the World Wars*, Macmillan, 1974, p 91.

3 John Maynard Keynes, "The economic consequences of Mr. Churchill," in *Essays in Persuasion*, 1931.

4 Milton Friedman and Anna J. Schwartz, *A Monetary History of the United States 1867–1960*, Princeton University Press, 1963.

5 Ellen R. McGrattan and Edward C. Prescott, *The 1929 Stock Market: Irving Fisher Was Right*, Federal Reserve Bank of Minneapolis, Research Department Staff Report No. 294, March 2003.

6 Chancellor, *op cit*, p 199.

7 Friedman and Schwartz, *op cit*.

8 Ben Bernanke, "Non-monetary effects of the financial crisis in the propagation of the Great Depression," *American Economic Review*, June 1983.

9 *International Bank Credit Analyst*, August 2002, p 16.

CHAPTER 3

1 M2 includes cash and bank deposits, while CDs are certificates of deposit, essentially fixed-term deposits, usually 30, 60, or 90 days.

2 All banks are required to meet these international standards, agreed under the auspices of the Bank for International Settlements, based in Basle. But while "capital" usually refers only to actual funds put up by the banks' owners, in Japan banks have been allowed to include their paper gains on stockholdings.

3 *OECD Economic Outlook 75*, Paris, June 2004.

4 B. R. Mitchell, *International Historical Statistics: The Americas and Australasia*, Macmillan, 1983.

5 Irving Fisher, "Debt Deflation Theory of Great Depressions," *Econometrica*, Vol. 1, pp 327–57, 1933.
6 For a good discussion see Ben Bernanke, "Deflation–making sure 'it' doesn't happen here," Speech before the National Economists Club, Washington DC, November 21st, 2002. Federal Reserve website www.federalreserve.gov.
7 See Mitsuhiro Fukao, *Financial Strains and the Zero Bound: The Japanese Experience*, BIS Working Papers No 141, September 2003.

CHAPTER 4

1 The US rules are complicated. For a good exposition see Gary Shilling, "Pension profits become corporate costs," *Business Economics*, October 2003, p 55.
2 *The Economist*, February 7th, 2004, pp 77–8.
3 *Financial Times*, April 21st, 2004, p 6.
4 *The Economist*, February 7th, 2004.
5 *Financial Times*, April 22nd, 2004, p 6.
6 *Financial Times*, April 21st, 2004, p 6.
7 For a full analysis see Felix Eschenbach and Ludger Schuknecht, "Budgetary risks from real estate and stock markets," *Economic Policy*, No. 39, July 2004, pp 315–46.
8 Some of the same problems that we have seen since the 1990s bubble burst appeared in the late 1980s and made the 1990–91 recession worse. Cuts in interest rates in 1987 (which were matched in other countries) played a role in inflating other asset markets, particularly property. Commercial property prices suffered a moderate bubble in the US and UK, while housing saw a dramatic bubble in the UK and in parts of the US, notably Boston and San Francisco. Low interest rates also fueled the management buyout fever, relying on heavy leverage.

CHAPTER 5

1 Capital Economics, reported in *The Economist*, November 29th, 2003, p 111.
2 J. Ayuso and F. Restoy, *House Prices and Rents: An Equilibrium Asset Pricing Approach*, Bank of Spain Working Paper, no. 0304, 2003.
3 *The Economist*, March 20th, 2004, p 85.
4 See for example Jonathan McCarthy and Richard W. Peach, "Are Home Prices the Next 'Bubble'?," *Economic Policy Review*, Federal Reserve Bank of New York, forthcoming.
5 Gregory D. Sutton, "Explaining changes in house prices," *BIS Quarterly Review*, September 2002.
6 *The Economist*, June 5th, 2002.

CHAPTER 6

1 For a full and detailed analysis see the "Barker Report," Kate Barker, *Delivering Stability: Securing our Future Housing Needs*, March 17th, 2004. Available at www.barkerreview.org.
2 www.ipdindex.co.uk.
3 Bank of England, *Financial Stability Review*, June 2000, pp 105–25.
4 CEBR, quoted in *The Business*, October 26th, 2003, p 2.
5 For the Barker Report see Note 1. David Miles' report, *The UK Mortgage Market: Taking a Longer Term View*, is available at www.hm-treasury.gov.uk/media//80DDf/miles04_470[1].pdf.

CHAPTER 7

1 John Krainer, "House price bubbles," *Economic Letter*, Number 2003-06, March 7th, 2003, Federal Reserve Bank of San Francisco. Looking at the house price to rental ratio, this study found an overvaluation relative to past averages of 11 percent, as of Q3 2002. This is slightly higher than the estimate from the Bank of Spain in Chapter 5. But given house price and rent trends since then, I estimate that this

overvaluation rose to about 20 percent by end 2003. Note that the house price index used in most studies and in this chapter is from OFHEO (Office of Federal Housing Enterprise Oversight). See www.ofheo.gov.

2 *Wall Street Journal*, January 27th, 2004, p D2.

3 Marc Labonte, *US Housing Prices: Is There a Bubble?*, Report for Congress, May 16th, 2003.

4 Benjamin Wallace-Wells, "There goes the neighborhood," *Washington Monthly*, April 2004.

5 Kenneth Harney, "The nation's housing: Appraisers pressed to over-value, study finds," *Detroit Free Press*, September 14th, 2003.

6 Labonte, *op cit.*

7 Richard Freeman, *Executive Intelligence Review Economics*, March 14th 2003. Available from www.larouchepub.com.

CHAPTER 8

1 The popular view of banks is that they take in deposits and then look for lending opportunities. In fact, banks manage both sides of their balance sheets. Many start by identifying lending opportunities and making loans. Then if they are short of deposits they simply borrow them on the wholesale market from other banks by paying the overnight interest rate. Other banks focus first on generating deposits, often the ones with a large retail base with lots of branches around the country. They will make their own loans too, but they sell surplus deposits to other banks through the overnight market.

    And the clever thing is that the assets of an individual bank and indeed the banking system as a whole (essentially loans together with securities such as bonds) match liabilities (deposits) fairly easily. This is because whenever somebody takes out a loan the money is either in their account or, if they buy something with it, it moves to someone else's account.

    Here is an example in more detail. Suppose a man takes out a loan from a bank. The first thing that happens is that the bank places the loan into his current account, ready to be spent. The bank's books show a liability (the deposit) and an equal asset (its claim on the borrower). The books are still balanced, but debt has increased. So has the national money supply, because it is the sum of all cash and bank deposits. Now suppose he uses the loan to buy a car. The money moves from his account to the dealer's account at another bank. His bank will then need to find another deposit from somewhere to keep its books balanced that night, but the dealer's bank will probably put the new deposit on to the wholesale market. So the banking system as a whole is once again easily balanced. While money whizzes in every direction during the day, when the books are closed every night it all balances.

2 For an exposition of the problems and risks see Peter Warburton, *Debt and Delusion: Central Bank Follies that Threaten Disaster*, Allen Lane/Penguin Press, 1999.

3 One of the main concerns of critics of the new proposals is that they could further encourage banks to be pro-cyclical in their lending and therefore make the risk of bubbles still greater in future.

4 The figures are approximate. In 1987 rates touched 7 percent briefly but they averaged 9.3 percent for the year. With a spread of 2 percent over base rates mortgage rates were about 11 percent in 1987. In 1990 official rates averaged 14.2 percent and, although mortgage spreads came down slightly, mortgage rates were up to nearly 16 percent. Overall then, mortgage holders faced a rise in interest payments of about 5 percent, which works out at about 45 percent in money terms.

5 *Inflation Report*, Bank of England, May 2004.

6 Chris Faulkner-MacDonagh and Martin Muhleisen, "Are US households living beyond their means?," *Finance and Development*, March 2004.

CHAPTER 9

1 McGrattan and Prescott, *op cit*.

2 Hans-Joachim Voth, *With a Bang not a Whimper: Pricking Germany's Stock Market Bubble in 1927 and the Slide into Depression*, CEPR Discussion Paper No. 3257, March 2002.

3   Peter Garber, "Famous first bubbles," *Journal of Economic Perspectives*, Vol. 4, No. 2, pp 35–54.

4   One of the earliest books on bubbles was Charles MacKay, *Extraordinary Popular Delusions and the Madness of Crowds*, 1841.

5   Daniel Kahneman and Amos Tversky, "Prospect theory: An analysis of decision under risk," *Econometrica*, 263–91, 1979.

6   G. B. Northcraft and M. A. Neale, "Experts, amateurs, and real estate: An anchoring-and-adjustment prespective on property pricing decisions," *Organizational Behaviour and Human Decision Processes*, Vol. 39, pp 84–97, 1987.

7   Robert J. Shiller, "Human behaviour and the efficiency of the financial system," in John B. Taylor and Michael Woodford (eds), *Handbook of Macroeconomics*, Elsevier, 1999.

8   Gary Belsky and Thomas Gilovich, *Why Smart People Make Big Money Mistakes and How to Correct Them: Lessons from the New Science of Behavioral Economics*, Simon and Schuster, 2000.

9   D. Ebrlich, I. Guttman, P. Schoenbach, and J. Mills, "Postdecision exposure to relevant information," *Journal of Abnormal and Social Psychology*, Vol. 67, pp 382–94, 1957.

10 Shiller, *op cit.*

11 Didier Sornette, *Why Stock Markets Crash: Critical Events in Complex Financial Systems*, Princeton University Press, 2003. For Professor Sornette's latest views on the markets see his website, www.ess.ucla.edu/faculty/sornette. As of early 2004 he was expecting renewed weakness in US stocks and saw a bubble in UK housing, though not in the US. For a popular introduction to the subject see Malcolm Gladwell, *The Tipping Point*, Abacus, 2000.

12 George Soros, one of the most successful investors of all time, developed the concept of "reflexivity," where changes in a market price feed back into the market itself. George Soros, *The Alchemy of Finance*, John Wiley, 1994.

CHAPTER 10

1 R. Balvers, Y. Wu, and E. Gilliland, "Mean reversion across national stock markets and parametric contrarian investment strategies," *Journal of Finance*, No. 55, pp 745–72, 2000. Campbell and Shiller, "Mean reversion in stock prices," *Journal of Financial Economics*, Vol. 22, 1988, pp 27–59.

2 Robert Shiller, *Irrational Exuberance*, Princeton University Press, 2000.

3 It is true that US stocks did not fall very much during the 1990 recession but showed more of a sideways pattern. Allowing for inflation, however, stocks were flat between August 1987 and February 1991. And the investor in bonds or cash would have still been ahead until 1993. Note that there have also been some occasions when the PE ratio was above 20 times because earnings were depressed by an economic slowdown and investors were expecting a rebound, for example 1992–3 and 2003.

4 James K. Glassman and Kevin A. Hassett, *DOW 36000: The New Strategy for Profiting from the Coming Rise in the Stock Market*, Times Books, 1999.

5 For an introduction see John Calverley, *Investors Guide to Economic Fundamentals*, John Wiley, 2003.

6 Elroy Dimson, Paul Marsh, and Mike Staunton, *Millennium Book II: 101 Years of Investment Returns*, London Business School and ABN AMRO. 2001.

7 Robert D. Arnott and Peter L. Bernstein, "What risk premium is normal?," *AIMR*, March/April 2002, pp 75–8, contains a rigorous examination of this argument.

8 US corporate bonds (and those of many other countries) are assigned ratings by the major ratings agencies (including Moodys, Standard and Poors, and Fitch). Government bonds as well as very good private-sector risks are rated AAA, then risk progressively rises through AA, A, to BBB–, all of which are rated as "investment grade." From BB+ down through B is rated speculative grade.

9 Standard and Poors, *Rating Performance 2001*, February 2002.

10 I have ignored the interest lost if the bonds default early in the 10-year period. If we take the extreme case where the 5.3 percent

cumulative default occurred the day after the portfolio was purchased, then the loss of interest would reduce the advantage somewhat, with the amount depending on the overall level of interest rates. At 6 percent interest rates the loss would be a further 2.4 percent.

11 R. Mehra and E. C. Prescott, "The equity risk premium: A puzzle," *Journal of Monetary Economics*, Vol. 15, 1985, pp 145–61.

12 Data for housing are much more difficult to assess than those for stocks. In principle, housing is believed to depreciate by 1–2 percent per annum. To some extent depreciation is captured in my figures for annual costs as the interior of the property is refurbished. But in many countries older buildings are discounted just because they are old. In Europe, of course, the reverse is often true. Another complication is that it is not clear to what extent house price indices are able to compensate for improvements in the quality of housing over time, for example the provision of central heating or air conditioning, so this further muddies the waters.

CHAPTER 11

1 This is of course not at all what free market economists would prescribe and some have been critical, both of the willingness to respond to stock market weakness with ultra-low rates and the tolerance of a bubble in house prices. But it is probably inevitable that governments will try to avoid big falls in asset prices, which makes it all the more relevant that they should also consider ways to limit the upside.

2 The Bank for International Settlements has taken a leading role in exploring these issues. See for instance Claudio Borio and Philip Lowe, *Asset Prices, Financial and Monetary Stability: Exploring the Nexus*, BIS Working Paper No. 114, July 2002 and Claudio Borio and William White, *Whither Monetary and Financial Stability? The Implications of Evolving Policy Regimes*, BIS Working Paper No. 147, February 2004. The *BIS Annual Report*, published each Spring, and the *BIS Quarterly Review* also regularly explore these themes.

3 Cecchetti claims, however, that the Fed did take the stock market boom into account to some extent and the argument should be about whether or not it did enough, not whether it reacted at all. Stephen G. Cecchetti, "What the FOMC says and does when the stock market booms," *RBA Annual Conference*, Vol. 2003-05, Reserve Bank of Australia, 2003.

4 See for example Stephen G. Cecchetti, Hans Genberg, and Sushil Wadhwani, *Asset Prices in a Flexible Inflation Targeting Framework*. paper prepared for the conference on Asset Price Bubbles: Implications for Monetary Regulatory and International Policies, organized by the Federal Reserve Bank of Chicago and the World Bank, Chicago, April 22–24th, 2002. Also Charles Bean, *Asset Prices, Financial Imbalances and Monetary Policy: Are Inflation Targets Enough?*, BIS Working Paper No. 140, September 2003.

5 Charles Goodheart, "What weight should be given to asset prices in the measurement of inflation?," *The Economic Journal*, June 2001, pp F335–56.

6 John Calverley, "Spotting the next asset price bubble," *Financial Times*, November 15th, 2002, p 19.

7 Adam Seitchik, *The Business*, June 22–23rd, 2003, p 18.

8 For an overview see *Turbulence in Asset Markets: The Role of Micro Policies*, OECD Contact Group Report, Paris, September 2002.

9 For a discussion see Anna J. Schwartz, *Asset Price Inflation and Monetary Policy*, NBER Working Paper No. 9321, November 2002.

10 Claudio Borio, *Towards a Macroprudential Framework for Financial Supervision and Regulation?*, BIS Working Paper No. 128, February 2003.

11 Fiona Mann and Ian Michael, "Dynamic provisioning: Issues and applications," *Bank of England Financial Stability Review*, December 2002.

12 See OECD *Contact Group Report*, p 23.

13 Barker. *op cit*.

14 See E. P. Davis, *Debt, Financial Fragility and Systemic Risk*, Oxford University Press, 1992, p 245.

CHAPTER 12

1 Investment Company Institute, quoted in *Financial Times*, October 31st, 2003.
2 To see how rebalancing works, imagine a portfolio at the start of the year with 50 percent in stocks and 50 percent in cash and bonds. During the year stocks soar 25 percent while the cash and bonds half earns just 5 percent. At the end of the year the portfolio will have 54.3 percent in stocks and only 45.7 percent in cash and bonds. By selling some stocks to bring them back to a 50 percent weighting investors are in effect taking profits on the upward move and increasing their holdings of bonds. Someone still adding to their portfolio each year through new savings may be able to achieve the same effect by putting the new money straight into cash and bonds rather than stocks.
3 As noted in Chapter 4, companies are under severe pressure if their pension fund is underfunded when its assets are "marked to market." Individuals can more easily afford to take the long view.
4 Roger Bootle makes this point very eloquently in *Money for Nothing*, Nicholas Brealey, 2003.

INDEX

1920s stock market bubble xii, 2, 25, 26–35, 58
1990s stock market bubble xii, 2–3, 25–6, 57–70

A

anchoring 127–9, 134
Asian crisis 1997 1, 3, 15, 31, 47, 93, 118, 179
asset price bubbles, strategies for 181–5
asset prices xi, 19-23, 26, 31, 37, 40–41, 50–53, 159, 162–5
Asset Valuation Committee (AVC) 167–70, 172, 175–6, 180, 182
Australia 107, 113, 159–60
Australia house prices xi–xii, 5, 15, 73, 81–2, 93, 199–200

B

bailout 179
bank lending xii, 6, 18, 34–5, 96, 108–10, 172–3
Bank of England 29, 30, 85, 87–8, 95, 114–15, 166, 177, 198

Bank of Japan 44–5, 48
Basle capital arrangements 45, 109–10
behavioral finance xii, 125–32, 136
bonds, valuation of 143–8
Brown, Gordon 96
bubbles
    1920s stock market xii, 2, 25, 26–35, 58
    1990s stock market xii, 2–3, 25–6, 57–70
    classic cars 6
    emerging market mining mania 1
    Impressionist paintings 6
    internet 13, 18
    Japan 1980s xii, xiii, 1, 41–56, 58
    Netherlands housing 5, 23, 73
    railway mania 1
    Scandinavia housing 1, 18, 23
    South Sea 1, 13
    Spain housing 5, 15, 23, 73, 81
    technology mania 1
    Tulip Mania 1
    UK housing xi–xii, 1, 15, 18, 23, 73, 83–96, 200

bubbles
  effects of 6
  housing xi–xiii, 2, 6, 15,
    185–7
  identifying 12–18
  importance of 6
  nonmonetary measures to
    control 171–2
  origins of xii, 6
  pathology of 123–36
  stages of 11–12
  strategies for 181–5
  theory of rational 132–3
  typical characteristics of
    12–18
  warnings of 166–70
budget deficits 4, 66–8, 159
Buffett, Warren 184
Bush, President George W. 4, 59
business cycle 37–8
buy-to-let funds 17

C

Canada 81
central banks xii, 5, 21, 47, 51,
  53, 165, 177–9, 196, 201
China 49, 197
Churchill, Winston 30
classic car price bubble 6
cognitive dissonance 131
company behavior 23–5
consumer expenditure deflator 30
consumer spending 19–22, 58,
  112–13

contrarianism 183–4
critical state theory 133–5
currency devaluation 54

D

debt deflation 50–52, 110
debt destruction 179–80
deflation xii, 3, 5, 42–56, 58,
  146, 192–3, 196
depression 1, 2, 58
Depression, Great 26–41, 49, 58
disaster magnification 131
disaster myopia 131
displacement 11
dollar weakness 4, 44

E

economic boom 11, 26
efficient markets hypothesis 123–5
emerging market mining mania
  1
endowment mortgages 64
equity risk premium 148–50
euphoria 1, 11, 109
exchange rates 18

F

Fannie Mae (Federal National
  Mortgage Corporation) 100–1,
  104–5, 180

Federal Reserve Board 28–35,
  59–60, 69, 106, 124, 163–5, 177
Felix, David xii
Financial Services Authority 35,
  167, 168
fiscal stimulus 4, 59
Fisher, Irving 32–3
FOMC 168
fools rallies 129
France 4, 23, 81
Freddie Mac (Federal Home Loan
  Mortgage Corporation) 100–1,
  104–5, 180
Friedman, Milton 32

Hoover, Herbert 30
house price–earnings ratio 14,
  16, 33, 57–8, 73, 86, 93,
  137–8, 140, 150, 169
house prices xi, 21–2, 26–7,
  40–41, 58, 70, 73–119, 151–2
house prices–rents 74
household debt xii, 5, 18,
  107–19, 200–1
household savings rate 18,
  20–21, 64–6, 79, 102
housing bubbles xi–xiii, 2, 6, 15,
  73–119
  strategies for 185–7

G

General Strike 31
Genghis Khan date test 127
Germany 4, 23, 73, 107
gold prices 6
Gold Standard 30–31, 33, 36–8,
  41, 44, 58, 177–8
Great Depression 26–41, 49, 58
Greenspan, Alan xi, 3, 26–7, 30,
  47, 57, 68–70, 103, 119, 165–6,
  169, 177, 180, 195
Greenspan put 52, 161

H

herd instinct 130–31
Hong Kong xi, 49–50, 58–9,
  173–4

I

Impressionist paintings price
  bubble 6
inflation xi, 4, 30, 43, 46–7,
  51–3, 59, 93, 114, 118, 153–8,
  163–5, 166, 179–80, 192–3,
  196–8
installment lending 29
interest rates xi, 4–5, 31, 34, 48,
  52–3, 68–9, 79–81, 95,
  115–19, 126, 140
internet bubble 13, 18
investors xi, xii, 1, 6, 17, 133
  strategies for xii, 181–94
Ireland 73, 81
irrational exuberance (*see also*
  Alan Greenspan) 57, 166, 169

J

Japan 4–5, 42, 73, 107
Japan 1980s bubble xii, xiii, 1,
    41–56, 58
Japan 1990s 1, 2–5, 59

K

Keynes, John Maynard 30
Kindleberger, Charles 1–2
King, Mervyn 96
Kuczynski, Michael xii

L

lender of last resort 12, 29,
    177
Long Term Capital Management
    (LTCM) 31, 35, 166, 177
loss aversion 126, 130

M

Macfarlane, Ian 82
mania 11
margin lending 34–5, 173
mean reversion 137–42
mental accounting 126
mental framing 126, 130
Meyer, Larry xii
Millennium Bug 31, 164
Minsky, Hyman xii

monetary policy xi. xii, 2–3,
    5–6, 13, 21, 26, 30–35, 37,
    52–6, 57–9, 79, 98–9, 106–19,
    159–80, 196, 201–2
and deflation 52–6
and household debt 107–19
mistakes xii, 2, 21, 58–9,
    115–16
new approaches 159–80
Monetary Policy Committee
    115–16, 168
mortgage equity withdrawal
    (MEW) 20, 78–0

N

Netherlands housing bubble 5,
    23, 73

O

OFHEO (Office of Federal Hous-
    ing Enterprise Oversight)
    104–5, 180
overconfidence 129
Overend Gurney 177
overoptimism 130

P

panic 12, 51
Pension Benefit Guarantee
    Corporation 62

pensions 23, 25, 60–64, 162,
  187–90
policy, monetary xi, xii, 2–3,
  5–6, 13, 21, 26, 30–35, 37,
  52–6, 57–9, 79, 98–9, 106–19,
  159–80, 196, 201–2
productivity 16–17, 29, 43, 119,
  201
prospect theory 125–7

R

railway mania 1
rational bubbles, theory of
  132–3
recession 1, 5, 15, 26, 32, 57
revulsion 12
risk premiums 141–2
Russian crisis 1998 31

S

Scandinavia housing bubble 1,
  18, 23
Securities and Exchange Commission 35, 180
September 11th, 2001 59, 130,
  177
Shadow Open Market Committee
  168
share prices (*see also* asset prices)
  23–5, 28–9
silver prices 6
slowdown 1, 12, 31, 33–4, 58

Smoot–Hawley tariff bill 38
South Sea Bubble 1, 13
Spain housing bubble 5, 15, 23,
  73, 81
speculation 16, 11–12, 17
Split Capital Trusts 35
stress test 193–4
Switzerland 73

T

technology mania 1
Tobin's Q 23–5
trade protectionism 2
Tulip Mania 1

U

UK 4, 61–3, 107, 113–16, 159
  housing bubble xi–xii, 1, 15,
  18, 23, 73, 83–96, 200
US xi–xii, 3–4, 14, 61–2, 107,
  113, 116–19, 159
  house prices 5, 73, 75–6,
  97–106

V

valuations xii, 1, 5–6, 11, 16, 33,
  57, 127–8, 136–58

W

wage cuts 49–50
Wall Street Crash 1–2, 25, 33–4,
    40
wealth effects 19–23
WhizzPizza 24–5